MIGRANT ANGELS

WHY TEACHERS QUIT THE SCHOOLS

by

DWIGHT EMERSON MITCHELL

Cover design by Jean Gates Hall,
Sacramento, California

Palo Alto, California
1968

Copyright 1968

by

Dwight Emerson Mitchell

Lithographed by Rosicrucian Press, Ltd.
76 Notre Dame Avenue, San Jose, California 95106

DEDICATION

To teachers, including my wife, Betty, who have undergone The Treatment, especially those who helped me obtain material for this book.

TABLE OF CONTENTS

ACKNOWLEDGMENTS

It is impossible to name all of the persons who have given me valuable help in writing this book; this is the unpleasant aspect of writing the Acknowledgments. I am indebted to more than 30 persons who read the manuscript and to scores of others who gave me their insights in my subject before and during the writing.

My wife, Betty, has been the mainspring, helping at every step with unflagging interest, insights more penetrating than mine, and inexhaustible tolerance.

Others I must name, all Californians but one, include Dr. and Mrs. Ernesto Galarza and George W. Sherman of San Jose, who have criticized, advised, and encouraged me constantly. I was helped by sage and stimulating comments of Ben Hitt of Santa Clara, J. Alvin Kugelmass of San Jose, and Vic Ulmer of Saratoga. Torrey and Florence Smith of Walnut Creek, Jack Owens of Redding, and Hugh and Elaine MacColl of Sacramento have never failed me on the numerous occasions when I have fled to them for counsel.

George Young of Pacifica gave me direction at a critical juncture. Maurice Englander of San Francisco and my niece, Barbara Kramer, of Ventura discerned a flaw which I have endeavored to rectify. For the past year Mr. Englander has been a frequent inspirer and gadfly, as needed, out of his hard-won spare time.

Professor Earl Vance of Tallahassee, Fla. kindly checked some facts and interpretations.

Always in the background, unobtrusive but of prime importance, have been the wise counsel and inspiring example of Ben Rust of Richmond. For a dozen years he and Dr. Galarza have been my Rock of Gibralter.

Florence Dixon of Santa Rosa and Marian Harrington of Menlo Park helped me generously in proof reading.

FOREWORD

What's wrong with education?

How many times have you heard that query?

And how many answers have you received, based on study, research, knowledge, or what have you?

Here is a clear, poignant, telling, and deep-seated explanation of what is wrong with education, based on EXPERIENCE. The author has been a newspaper reporter, a student, and a high school and college teacher of Journalism and English. He has seen things from the inside, as a teacher and an author. He has seen things from the other side, reporting educational news for the SAN JOSE MERCURY AND NEWS, for eight years.

His wife was one of the best known elementary teachers in the county, a woman of sensitivity who has endured much for her children in the classroom, who has given them enduring values as an educator. And now, both having retired, Mr. Mitchell has put down on paper reasons, through experiential analogy, through searing experience, why education has so often floundered, so often destroyed children instead of strengthening them, so often devastated sensitive teachers instead of nourishing them.

Years ago, when I first started to teach, in 1939, we called the teachers who moved around from district to district 'suitcase teachers.' It was the common practice then, during the depression, to subvert the tenure law by moving teachers about every third year. According to the law, any teacher who received a fourth annual contract in California automatically received tenure. So good teachers were traded from district to district every fourth year. They never had a permanent job. They couldn't hope to. Tenure was an illusion, reserved for a very few favorites.

To this day a young teacher can expect to be tested, tried, and sent off with his suitcase, especially if he displays erudition, intelligence, and independence. The 'suitcase teacher,' it is true, has largely dwindled, because of teacher shortages and the population explosion. But, he has not disappeared. And the very good teachers must keep their guards up. For the basic distrust of the scholar, the intellectual, and the independent teacher still remains in administrative circles.

Mr. Mitchell's 'migrant angel' is still a migrant, still flitting about EN LIMBO, still asking for the privilege of dispensing knowledge, still distrusted. Nevertheless, the educator will still make studies and look for novel solutions to education. Although the solution is the simple one, the one which respects and dignifies the teacher, it is all too simple for those who prop up the establishment rather than furthering quality in education.

Years ago the deceased Clair Engle, California's senator, ran for the United States Senate on a water program. And he said, and I paraphrase him: 'Let us stop making water studies and do something about water. Every study seems to prove the same thing, namely, that water runs down hill.'

Ben Rust
Richmond, Calif.

PREFACE

This book is one man's personal report on a supposed mystery which is not a mystery at all, the inability of schools to attract and hold their best teachers.

The output of graduates of teacher training institutions is far greater year after year than the number of teaching jobs available. I doubt that half of these credentialed graduates ever teach at all. Only a few make teaching a career. This strikes me as a prodigal waste. Such has been the situation during all of my adult years. School people constantly bemoan it.

Not to my knowledge however have they defined the reasons the schools cannot hold enough good teachers. The reasons are clear why teachers leave even though they love learning and working with the young in the pursuit of learning. I count myself one of these.

This problem was not on the agenda of the National White House Conference on Education in 1965. Ten years earlier, in the 1955 conference, it was one of the main items of discussion. It was suggested that the cause may lie in working conditions. I thought it would have been profitable to look more deeply into this; for instance, to have specified and analyzed one or several working conditions that might discourage teachers.

Certainly it was discouraging working conditions that compelled me to give up classroom teaching. As a newspaper writer, especially after the teaching years, I continued to observe so many instances of harsh and inconsiderate treatment of school workers that I felt the entire subject should be brought into open examination; there are certain employment conditions tolerated in few other occupations.

My notebook began accumulating information of incidents verifying this until I had a good-sized collection of case studies. A newspaper published a series of articles which I produced from these notes. Cases came to my notice from far and near. Teachers sought me out to relate their grievances. One teacher very close to my personal life was subjected to the same mistreatment I observed elsewhere.

I thought a book would help citizens, who own the schools and support them for the education of their children, to be informed. Two points became apparent. First, many case studies would be merely repetitious. There is a pattern in all of them such that when teachers came to tell me their grievances I already knew, to their astonishment, a good part of what they were about to relate. Second, the causes of unfavorable conditions require considerable exposition of the school organizational structure and management practices.

I have chosen not to identify individuals in the case studies, giving all of them fictional names instead, to avoid building sympathy for individuals but rather to present the pattern of working conditions of all teachers. In addition, some of my information is confidential. One specific case is more illuminating than a vast amount of generalization. Solving a problem is in one respect like getting married or becoming a parent--it is not done in general but in particular.

My examples cover a wide span of years for cause--to demonstrate that the problem is an old one and it remains substantially unchanged. It is as old as the public schools themselves. My cases touch five decades of my own observation, from the 1920's to the mid-1960's.

Poor working conditions and personnel practices are in my view the root flaw of the schools; hence the scope of this book is broad; for analysis of the root flaw reveals that multitudes of other problems are merely derivative. Correct the major flaw and the derivative ones vanish. Destroy the poisonous root and the evil branches wither and die.

On one point I take a defensive position which I here state as explicitly as I can, once for all. This book is critical-- some may feel harshly so--of certain practices of school management with relation to teachers. This would be rank ungraciousness if the only consideration were my almost uniformly friendly relations with school men--administrators, teachers, trustees. Indeed, there is not today a single school person against whom I feel any hostility for anything that happened in my relations with him as a newspaper writer or teacher.

Yet I do not abate one jot or tittle of what this book contains. My criticism is against practices, not persons. The harshness is in the practices, not in me for stating them.

Finally, I have taken great care that my factual material is beyond challenge. Citizens ought to give continuous attention and thought to the education of the young. My purpose is to provide information on what I regard as the most crucial flaw of the schools.

Chapter 1

THE UNWILLING OVERSUPPLY

This country has had a great oversupply of qualified school teachers for years, but always a scarcity of experienced, able teachers in the classrooms. This was already an old problem when I first taught school in 1920. It has continued to this day.

Why? This question has been raised a million times and discussed with puzzled shaking of heads; but no satisfactory answer has come forth. Meanwhile, the burgeoning teacher training centers have continued producing far more new minted teachers each year than the schools can possibly employ.

Great numbers of the annual crops of graduates never teach at all. After receiving degrees and teaching credentials, they immediately turn to occupations other than teaching. Large numbers who do accept teaching jobs leave after a year or a few years. School people know that many of these are young women who make teaching an interlude between graduation and marriage. This leaves the basic problem unresolved-- why the schools do not attract more people to make teaching a career.

It is my conviction that this unfortunate situation can be explained; that indeed its basis is rather simple, lying in working conditions and personnel practices. School employment has always been an unstable job. Teachers are migrant workers, a highly discouraging situation for a career.

They cannot afford this and the more independent ones will not abide it. This unsettled state destroys much of a teacher's effectiveness and it is an insult to the dignity of this greatest of occupations. It is an intolerable economic burden especially for teachers with families to support.

The conditions that make teachers migrants are the substance, then, of this book.

I was one of the migrant teachers for 21 years. My teaching ended in 1947. Thirteen years later, in 1960, in a conversation I had with a middle aged man who had once been a school principal in rural areas for years, he stated the case of migrancy succinctly.

'In your first year in a school district,' he said, 'you can do no wrong. In the second year, they choose up sides; the third year, they give you the axe.'

'They' in his meaning are the school boards and community citizens. The course of a school man's job tenure which he stated so concisely often runs its sequence in only one year or two instead of the three he gave it. Many thousands of teachers and former teachers will instantly recognize the sequence. A few words of reminder will go far to state the situation. Parents and trustees all too often nurse a mental image of an impossibly ideal teacher. She is a person, or rather an Angel, preferably beautiful, with magic powers to make over the community's youngsters in the image of the parents' hearts' desires.

When these parental fantasies come to their inevitable collision with reality, the parents vent their frustrations on the teacher, sending her packing on her migrant way. Thereupon they resume the search for a paragon of more than mortal power to beat knowledge into the reluctant young and make them learn their manners.

If the teacher does not want to be fired after she has lost favor, what can she do? Nothing. She can appeal, of course, but only to the persons firing her. This is an individual bargaining situation for her in which her only protection is her power of persuasion. No objective person with understanding would argue that this is any real protection of a teacher's or any employe's job.

The teacher's job security status is on a level with that of the farm worker, domestic help, the nurse, and many white collar workers. Contrast this with the situation of millions of labor union members, and millions of public employes of the Federal Government, the 50 states, and cities and counties whose jobs are protected by civil service and often by unionization as well.

An employer who undertakes to dismiss a union member or civil service employe knows that he will have serious trouble

2

unless he has strong evidence that the employe deserves to be separated from his job. Union members will leap on the instant to the defense of a threatened or beleaguered brother.

There is no such support, nor has there ever been, for a teacher, except the relatively few who are unionized. There is no civil service for teachers. The National Education Association and its many state, regional, and local subdivisions and affiliates have machinery for taking part in personnel disputes among their members, such as a disputed dismissal of a teacher. I have observed their operations in this many times and shall relate some of the cases. In no sense could I feel that their activities protect teachers.

My evidence to the contrary looms large in this writing; for example, the cases of Teachers Harry Elliott, Everett Charles, Alice Adams, and others. These names, as I explained in the preface, are fictional, as are all I shall mention. All are actual persons and all of my factual statements about them are true facts. I have usually but not always referred to them by their actual gender.

Teacher Charles, who was being harassed by his superintendent, gave early notice of his resignation. The superintendent, whom I am calling Grover Smith, refused to accept it. Teacher Charles thereupon appealed to the teachers' association of his State for help. He wrote, 'They promised their field representative would contact me. He never did but instead talked with the trouble makers. I finally talked with him when Miss----invited me to her house for a meeting, and I could quickly see we were boring him and would get no help from him.'

Of all public institutions, schools are closest to the hearts of adults, because of the deep involvement of the young. Hence people are easily aroused emotionally over school matters. Perhaps this emotional involvement accounts for the fantasies that teachers ought to have magic powers, like Angels, over the young. Emotion is clearly implied in the 'choose up sides' phrase a few pages back. Emotion is often involved in the dismissal of a teacher.

All this along with the lack of any restraint against exercise of the power to dismiss assuredly goes far to explain the instability of a teacher's job. For this many persons quit teaching in discouragement or disgust after being fired a few times, or even once. This very instability generates still greater instability by putting it in people's minds to become teachers who do not intend to continue more than a year

3

or two, especially between graduation from college and choice of a permanent occupation. Thus the instability, like other evils, grows by what it feeds on.

School people have looked year after year with concern over the incalculable loss in this constant turnover of teaching staffs. Annual reports of the National Education Association have shown a loss of some eight percent of certificated school workers each year. This is in addition to the loss of the large numbers of teachers' college graduates each year who do not even teach at all. The tragedy in all this is the loss suffered by the young, in low standards of education resulting from the constant turnover of personnel.

In my more than 50 years of close connection with the schools, the shortage of good teachers has been continuous, and constantly remarked upon with regret. How can we get enough good teachers and keep them? This is an enduring question. Teachers' colleges turn out more than twice as many graduates as are needed, if only they would remain available.

As school districts have grown larger in enrollment through the years, with population growth, urbanization, and district consolidations, instability of teaching jobs has continued under changed conditions but without improvement. This growth has been marked by the rise of school administration to a position of dominance.

Teachers find themselves no longer in direct contact with the trustees. Administration is interposed between them in a line and staff chain of command. A system of administrative rules and procedures has replaced the simple direct confrontation of teacher and board in the old days of the one-room school district. This new system becomes increasingly complex as districts become larger and larger. Administration and supervision have proliferated. The superintendent has a corps of staff officers and assistants; administration is separated from the district's schools in its own building; line officers called principals administer the various schools. In many, perhaps most schools, the principals have assistants.

In addition to all this are other workers both in the central administration building and in the administrative center of each school. These include not only secretaries, bookkeepers, and typist-stenographers, but also certificated specialists of many titles and functions--curriculum developers and revisers, consultants, coordinators, counselors, audio-

4

visualists, attendance supervisors, nurses, dental hygienists; there are specialists in speech, reading, mathematics, sciences, music, art, physical education, and other fields.

Many of these specialists have authority over the teachers, including the duty of reporting to the administration their judgment of the teacher's competence and his weaknesses and strengths. Theoretically, these certified non-teaching persons are expected to help the teachers. Teachers do not regard them as an unmixed blessing. Teachers are fearful of criticizing, for easily perceived reasons which will be referred to later in this book; anyone having the confidence of some classroom teachers will find that many of them regard some of the above specialists, especially supervisors and coordinators, with feelings ranging from dislike to much stronger aversions.

In this proliferation and increasing complexity, the classroom teacher finds himself beset on every hand with administrative rules and procedures and with the demands of supervisors and other officials on his time and energies. The dominant administration, interposed between teachers and trustees, directs teachers' activities, sometimes in minute details. The role of the Board is reduced largely to mere ratification of administrative recommendations, particularly as to personnel and educational philosophy and practice. Most of the Board's active role is in such matters as budgets, taxes, capital outlay, and operation of the physical plant.

Administration views the curriculum, or the studies the youngsters are required to pursue, and such matters as teaching methods and philosophy, as the province of the professional educators, rather than of the trustees and citizenry. As this view has gained wide acceptance, the administration has gained greater control over the schools and the destinies of teachers. It is rash to assume that the administrator will use this power to protect teachers from dissatisfied board members or other citizens. There are powerful forces impelling him another way.

He, like teachers, is vulnerable to the displeasure of trustees and citizens. The superintendent is most vulnerable of all. Uneasy lies the head that wears a crown. The public identifies him with the school system. He has to maintain a proper 'image' in the public eye. Always there are rivals or potential rivals for his position of power as head of a big organization.

All of these facts about school administration and particularly the superintendent are of the utmost importance to the security of teachers. Readers should keep clearly in mind-- since all school people are inclined at times to call themselves teachers--that administrators do not teach. Nor are the supervisors, coordinators and the other school workers such as those whose titles have been mentioned, regular classroom teachers. The teachers outnumber all of the other certified persons combined, by about seven and a half to one, and they do the basic work for which the schools exist. Whatever service the others render, the basic essential work of education is centered in the classroom, in the person of the classroom teacher.

It is easy to deduce from this why administration, and especially the superintendent, will get rid of many teachers regardless of the quality of their work. A very important reason for this is that the superintendent's security requires employes who owe their jobs to him, not to his predecessors.

The superintendent must be alert to the possibility that his position may be undermined by the rise to prominence of his subordinates. Many young teachers are ambitious for administrative posts. Any employe, even a classroom teacher, who becomes a leader in school or community affairs, is a potential threat. Such prominence may weaken the superintendent's position even if the teacher does not aspire to administration; for it diverts part of the public attention from the superintendent. He must quell dissent. He must stand firm against deviation from the educational philosophy he establishes in the district. He must mark for disfavor any teacher who attracts attention by individualistic behavior or eccentricity. Often the most brilliant and effective teachers have these characteristics.

The superintendent also marks for strong disfavor teachers who practice or defend teaching theories and methods which do not fit his program. He is careful, in hiring and promotion, to select persons who will support his policies. Thus a change of superintendents is a time of crisis for all employes. The new superintendent, especially if he is from outside the district, knows he can be undermined by teachers and other subordinates who are loyal to or owe preferment to his predecessor.

He employs means to give these persons a desire to leave. His position becomes more secure when he replaces them with his own appointees. Another frequently used tactic is to dissolve closely knit groups, such as teaching staffs of indivi-

6

dual schools, by scattering their members to different schools in the district.

Also of long-established use is the practice known among experienced workers in all occupations of making an unwanted employe's situation unpleasant by harassing tactics. Later in this book I shall specify a number of these tactics which I have observed in the schools. They are practically endless; unpleasant manner and tone of voice in greeting or conversation; discrimination at every small and large opportunity, faint praise, failure to provide classroom supplies, unpleasant assignments, etc. I have known some superintendents who seemed adept with all of these tactics. Teachers on tenure are just as vulnerable as the others, as one of the case studies in this book shows.

The tactics of advancing one's own purpose by trampling on other persons are prevalent in all walks of life. This book is concerned with how these tactics affect teachers, and how they discourage competent persons from accepting jobs as teachers and choosing teaching as a career.

It is easier to use these tactics in schools than in most other fields of employment, partly because the right of employers to hire and fire school employes has never been seriously challenged or modified.

At this point, another element requires attention, one that shows the teacher's plight to be much worse than I have so far shown. There is some conflict among educators over two theories of the relationship between administrators and teachers. The older theory is that they are all on some kind of hazy equality as colleagues. The other is that the school management--that is, the administration and board of trustees-- is in full charge of managing the district and therefore has the prerogative of directing everything, including the disposal of employes-- hiring them, directing their work, and firing them.

In what seems to be an effort to reconcile these two irreconcilables, certain formalities are observed in a dismissal, including a statement by the administration of the reasons. This statement is made by an administrator and the board accepts it and ratifies the dismissal.

Readers may realize at this point that teachers have indeed a precarious hold on their jobs. They may think this explains well enough why persons of independent spirit turn

7

away from teaching. They will see after an examination of the character of the dismissal statements which are often made that the case is actually much stronger than I have yet presented it. The case is more convincing still when it becomes clear that these statements, or accusations, are traditionally accepted by the board without supporting evidence.

As to the nature of the statements, I shall cite some that are subjective judgments made by administrators who have not gained their information first hand by observing the accused teacher at work. Some accusations are trivial, such as that Teacher Freda George ate potato chips in the classroom, and that Teacher Murray Quentin permitted his high school students to read John Steinbeck's GRAPES OF WRATH. Some accusations are stupid as well as trivial, such as that against a teacher whom the visiting administrator censured because he saw strands of thread on the floor. She had just finished giving her class of mentally retarded youngsters a sewing lesson.

Chapter 2

MEET THE SPOTTED COW

There is a French story of the time of the French Revolution about a poor wandering peasant who was brought into court after languishing in prison for more than a year without knowing why he had been deprived of his freedom. He was finally told that he was accused of owning a spotted cow. His vehement denial only incited the judge to fury and the attendent mob to a thirst for his blood. He was summarily sentenced to 50 years in prison and the guards hauled him out of court with difficulty and danger through the howling mob to the safety of his cell.

This preposterous accusation with the equally preposterous sequel which ruined the life of poor Jim the Wanderer, in Octave Mirbeau's story, is strikingly like many of the proceedings of school management against teachers; marked by the same unquestioning acceptance of mere accusation, whether serious or trivial, as its own evidence, proving guilt. This chapter, then, relates the story of a teacher accused of owning a spotted cow and simultaneously convicted and punished on no other ground than the accusation. The case is not unique. It is not even unusual.

This book is not concerned with teacher dismissals justified by proof of valid cause such as incompetence, irresponsibility, or dereliction of duty. It is concerned with willful, irresponsible dismissals, which have always abounded in many schools. It is concerned with the conditions giving rise to this pattern and with the circumstances and actions leading up to the dismissals.

Some of the tactics and willful, unprovable, trivial causes given for depriving teachers of their jobs have been mentioned. I offer here a few more examples of actual cases:

That Teacher Murray Quentin 'tossed the last drops of tea

9

from his cup on the schoolroom floor.'*

That Teacher Russell Roberts was blackballed by a member of an evaulating committee of three unidentified fellow teachers for reasons which, the superintendent was quoted as saying, were 'nothing you could put your finger on.'

That Teacher Alden Henry was too enthusiastic.

That Teacher Alice Adams wrote a nasty letter to her school board chairman when in fact there was no such letter.

That Teacher Leon Isaacs spoke too fast in leading his class in the daily pledge of allegiance to the flag.

Teacher Hazel Kelly was held culpable because two women complained to each other about her. (This suggests the question whether teachers are the only persons held responsible for complaints made behind their backs.)

Newspapers quoted a school board member as saying of Teacher Isaacs, 'He taught on cloud seven and in high school you should teach only on cloud five.'

These absurdities no doubt deserve the derision and scornful laughter which I assume they provoke; but readers may not want to dismiss them merely with laughter. The accusation of owning a spotted cow was equally ridiculous, but it was also terrible. In the one case a man's life was wrecked; in the others, teachers' careers were destroyed, their fellow teachers were muzzled and cowed, and unknown thousands of youngsters are poorer.

In 1961, the California Legislature enacted a law permitting a probationary teacher to demand a hearing on the causes of his dismissal. In June, 1963, my wife, Betty, and I attempted with only partial success to attend such a hearing. Prior to enactment of this law we had had experience with hearings in similar disputes, such as that for Teacher Wilma Floyd, which school boards had granted voluntarily. These were disorderly affairs, in which individuals were permitted to express their partisan views and prejudices and opinions, and give vent to their emotions.

However, this hearing for Teacher Isaacs clearly demon-

*Memorandum Decision No. 77549, Department No. 5, Superior Court, State of Calif., San Joaquin County, May 20, 1963.

strated that the law mentioned above at least effected some improvement. The procedure was orderly. There was recognition that evidence is required to support accusations. This I had not previously observed in teacher dismissals; for accusations had always been accepted without question. This may seem strange to readers but it is true. It seems to stem from the prerogative of the employer to dispose of an employe whenever he chooses; for this being the case, it matters little what reason he gives; any reason is the equivalent of 'I don't like you any more; go away.'

With all the improvements, nonetheless, the June, 1963 hearing still fell short of a thorough and impartial search for justice. The School Board chose to hold the hearing in a courtroom accommodating not more than one-third of the crowd. School boards often complain, and quite rightly, about the lack of public interest in school affairs. This exclusion certainly discouraged public interest and confidence. School management is happier when the public becomes interested in school affairs that show management in a favorable light.

Teacher Isaacs was fired after three years in a high school district. If he had been rehired he would have had tenure. He was accused of violating administrative orders that during an air raid drill he must require his students to lie under their desks; of arriving late to school; of being late in unlocking his classroom door; of not submitting acceptable lesson plans; of speaking too fast in leading the daily pledge of allegiance to the flag; and of not keeping a seating chart of his classes.

The courtroom seated 80 persons. The hearing continued for eleven hours, from 7:30 p.m. to 6:30 the following morning. There were occasional five- and ten-minute recesses. Betty and I were among the more than 200 persons who waited outside. The crowd dwindled slowly; at 3:30 a.m. we were able to find standing room in the hearing room. Witnesses testified under oath. They included several administrators and possibly some teachers for the prosecution and a number of fellow teachers, students, and others for Teacher Isaacs.

I heard none of the testimony for plaintiff and only part of that for the defense. This is not important, for whether or not the accusations were proved is of no material import to my present purpose. The relevant matters are the manner in which the hearing was conducted, particularly the roles of accuser, accused, and judge; and the relevancy of the accusations to teaching and learning.

I heard a few snatches of Isaacs' long turn on the witness

11

stand when I finally got a foot in the hearing room after nine hours' waiting outside. His demeanor was of special interest to me because there had been persistent reports that he was difficult to deal with. It was said that persons who recommended him to the employers who were now in process of casting him off had warned that he might be difficult at times though he was an extraordinarily good teacher.

I thought fractious tendencies might appear in him under the strain of cross examination. However, during my observation, he remained calm and objective. In talking with him at some length before this hearing, I received the impression that he could be fiercely impatient with trivia and cant, and that I regard as a virtue. Restless energy he had in abundance, and youth. Yet in testifying at length on the trivial accusations he spoke simply to the point, positively and without fear. I wondered if he felt embarrassment, as I did, that adults--and community leaders at that--should spend enormous energy and time on such tiny absurdities.

The hearing was made to resemble a trial, though of course it was in no sense a trial. The President of the Board of Trustees occupied the judge's chair. The jury box was reserved for the other four trustees. This left eight vacant jury seats, though all other seats and standing room were packed. Plaintiffs and defendant and their counsel sat as in a trial, immediately in front of and facing and below the level of the bench.

This court-like atmosphere did not escape notice during the hearing. Teacher Isaacs' attorney characterized the board's attitude as that of a 'kangaroo court.' After a board member repeatedly alluded to school district officials as 'our witnesses,' the attorney said, 'I was under the impression that this was to be an impartial hearing, but I am beginning to get the feeling that the jury is stacked.' He declared that the teacher was being tried by the same persons who had committed the dismissal which his teacher client complained was unjust.

The district attorney sat beside the board president and took a dual part in the proceedings. He advised the presiding board president on proper legal procedures, and he took over the role of judge himself when it became necessary to umpire disputes between the two attorneys. One of these, counsel for the school management, was one of the district attorney's own deputies.

This was essentially an individual bargaining situation. Teacher Isaacs' employers had fired him and he was attempt-

12

ing to prove to them that he did not deserve this treatment. Some school officials will deny that this was individual bargaining. They will assert that the administration had fired the teacher and the School Board was acting as an impartial intermediary between the administration and the teacher employe. This won't wash; first, because administration considers itself as representative of the teachers before the board and is therefore not the antagonist of the teachers; second, the board had implicated itself wholly on the side of the administration before the hearing was held, by accepting the recommendation for dismissal and by public statements. This is what school boards usually do in cases of dismissals. It was the board president who spoke of teaching on 'cloud seven.' Now, a few weeks later, he was playing the role of 'judge' in the hearing. I think the phrase 'playing the role' is correct. This was not a trial, it was play-acting like a trial; that is, it was make-believe, on cloud six perhaps.

Involvement of the district attorney's office aptly fit this individual bargaining situation. It was a function of this office in this particular county to act as counsel for other county public bodies. As this was a hearing under procedures prescribed by law, it seemed to me surprising that nobody raised a question of the propriety of the district attorney's adjudicating disputes between the attorneys when one of them was his own deputy, representing the office he held.

The fact that this legal hearing ended with Teacher Isaacs' dismissal is clear evidence, if any is needed, that there is nothing in law giving a teacher a right to a job. Teacher Isaacs' competence in the classroom was never in question. He had been recommended as one of the best teachers in California. His students were enthusiastic about him. In a petition of 75 students for his reinstatement they said he 'has shown us what education can be, and we want more of it, not less.'

Parents and college professors pleaded that students should continue to have the benefit of Teacher Isaacs' instruction. A mother said, 'He does more than pass knowledge on to his students; he teachers them to think for themselves.' A college teacher said he thought the school 'would want the best teachers it can get.'

A letter to the trustees, signed by 45 district citizens, protested the smallness of the hearing room in these words: 'At the heart of the issue seems to be a feeling on your part that the court can provide the orderly atmosphere essential to the

13

hearing. We suggest, though, that such an atmosphere could be maintained while insuring the right of the people to know. These are the people you represent. It is their money you spend. It is their right you must recognize.'

It is natural to ask why all the statements in behalf of Teacher Isaacs failed to move the school management. There is a clue, possibly the main clue, in the accusations: they are all concerned with the details of administrative machinery. Teacher Isaacs did not deny the accusation of occasionally being late to school and to his classes; he did testify that many teachers and administrators were occasionally late. He identified one of these, an administrator who he said not only came late but falsified the time of his arrival. He proposed that this person be questioned under oath. This suggestion was summarily rejected on the ground that this person was not the one accused.

Here is a particular kind of justice, to-wit, that when many are guilty, one is singled out to be accused and punished and the rest go scot free. A multiplicity of trivial administrative rules makes this system of selective justice and punishment convenient for the persons in power.

Teacher Isaacs said that during his three years' employment in that school district nobody ever told him when he was expected to be at the school. He learned this by observing when the others arrived. He said the administration had rejected all the lesson plans he submitted but had refused to specify what would be acceptable, despite his repeated requests.

This requirement that a teacher write his lesson plans and give them to an administrator such as a department head or principal is an administrative device defended on two basic points: 1. The plan shows whether the teacher is doing an acceptable job; 2. The plans are needed by the substitute who takes the class when the teacher is absent.

These two points clearly show the usefulness of lesson plans for helping the administration keep a tight rein on teachers, but their value in fostering learning is another matter. One of the most persistent complaints of teachers is the burden of non-teaching duties. All good teachers certainly make plans; written plans help a teacher if he makes them for his own use. They are an onerous burden when arbitrarily required regardless of the teacher's needs.

The idea that plans are necessary for a substitute is based

14

on current educational theory that the material assigned to students is to be pre-determined on a day-to-day basis and that any deviation from this lockstep pattern is disastrous.

This lockstep, in which all pupils are theoretically supposed to learn the same fixed dosages of knowledge at the same time day after day, has been defended by almost all school officials other than teachers with whom I have discussed educational practice since the early 1950's. Curiously, in all of my previous years of close association with schools, longer ago than 1920, this same lockstep was universally abhorred as the worst possible situation for learning. The classic example of it at its worst was frequently cited: The Minister of Education for France in some earlier age was said to have declared proudly that at any minute of any day in the school year, he could state exactly what every child in France was doing.

I find it hard to understand how the educators in America could have reversed themselves completely, and come back to this same lockstep, which conceives that pupils must be manipulated, in the intricate processes of learning, as though they were inert material like clay, wood, or iron.

With regard to the air raid drill, Teacher Isaacs testified that he had informed his pupils of their legal right to decide according to their consciences whether or not to assume the fetal position under their desks.

I did not hear the testimony on Teacher Isaacs' alleged sin of omission in not having a seating chart. I inquired with some diligence about this and gained the information that a seating chart is a drawing showing which classroom seat each pupil occupies; but I was unable to obtain any coherent idea whatever of the relevance of such a chart to the pursuit of learning.

I do not know by what prescience administration perceives that Young Junior will prosper in the acquisition of knowledge as long as he sits in the fourth seat of Row 5, but that should he ever occupy the sixth seat of Row 2 he is ruined forever.

The accusation that Teacher Isaacs made his pupils recite the Pledge of Allegiance to the Flag too rapidly was supported by a district administrator who said he had timed this ritual at 8.7 seconds. This was another accusation on which I was unable to hear the testimony. I have found that I can speak the Pledge with relative comfort at that speed. If there is a valid standard of speed in reciting these words, established by competent authority, the fact has assuredly not been made general knowledge.

15

This brief summary shows, I think, that the clue to the ouster of Teacher Isaacs is that priority is given to regulations and procedures of administration rather than to teaching and learning. Even Teacher Isaacs' principal, who played a key part in building the case against him, had earlier declared that if Teacher Isaacs' vigor could be diluted among the rest of the faculty, it would raise the interest of all students. The petitions of parents and students; the testimony of college professors and fellow teachers, were brushed aside. The words of a student who said Teacher Isaacs had 'opened a new world to me; I got interested in thoughts, and theories, and ideas,' were unavailing.

Many persons expended enormous energy to achieve the dismissal. There is no way of estimating the man-hours of labor devoted to this case by highly paid public officials in devising and supporting such picayune accusations as, for example, speaking the Pledge of Allegiance allegro instead of andante, and in solemnly debating and haggling over this trivia, and taking 11 hours of testimony over it.

Many thousands of teachers read about this case. All of them should have realized--and many did realize--that a similar fate could befall them at any time. Two of Teacher Isaacs' fellow teachers, both his close friends, left their jobs the same year he was fired. One of them--call him Teacher Newton Donald--was fired. The other, Teacher Herman Upton, resigned in protest of the treatment of Teacher Isaacs.

A teacher in a neighboring school district who was also an official of the American Federation of Teachers, AFL-CIO, commented that for each teacher who left the schools because of what happened to Teacher Isaacs, 'there are ten more who will stay out.' He may have been thinking of the large percentage of the annual crop of teachers' college graduates who never consider applying for teaching jobs at all.

Why did the school officials, in closed ranks, and the school trustees and county counsel's office all collaborate in such a performance as this, in an actual courtroom, giving with external apparatus the similitude of an objective judicial procedure, but without the substance? I cannot answer that, unless they confused acting the part--play acting--with reality. This is equivalent to presenting a play in which the villain is convicted of a murder, and then after the play is ended, sending to the gas chamber the actor who played the villain's part. God help the teacher who looks for justice from persons who set out to play act and be real at the same time.

Chapter 3

THE INCIDENT OF THE COPPER PLATES

Teacher Isaacs' loss of his job and the manner in which it was accomplished were in no sense out of the ordinary among teachers except for the hearing and the publicity. The right of school administrators and trustees to dismiss teachers and other employes at will is unqualified except for the minority of teachers who have tenure. (They have other means of getting rid of tenure teachers.)

This prerogative has continued with little modification since the beginning of public education in the United States. The same prerogative was originally held by management in all fields, both public, such as the postal service, and private, such as mining and manufacturing. In most fields, however, it was modified many years ago, in private industry by unions and in public employment by unions and civil service.

There is no civil service for teachers and only a few of them have union protection. Unionism has made some headway among teachers, notably since 1960, in a few large cities; but this involves only a small percentage of all the nation's teachers. With this small exception a teacher has a job only for the duration of his or her one-year contract or agreement of employment.

The manner of dismissal of Teacher Isaacs is an example of a practice peculiar to the schools of giving reasons for dismissal unsupported by evidence and often as nit-picking as those against Teacher Isaacs. This job insecurity in the schools is closely related to the historic and fiercely fought issue of an employe's right to a job versus the employer's right to complete freedom in the conduct of his business. This struggle originated in the industrial revolution before the public schools came into existence. It has a direct bearing on the insecure job status of teachers. It developed as an issue when the economy of western countries was shaped by

17

the industrial revolution which began in the Eighteenth Century.

Before the industrial revolution most persons in Colonial America were self-employed, the greater part of them in agriculture; moreover, they owned the land they farmed. Though they endured the extreme hardships of pioneering, they at least had the means of procuring the necessities of life by exerting themselves. The 'sacred' right of private property protected them from losing this resource against their wills. Nobody could wilfully or arbitrarily take their land away from them.

With the coming of the industrial revolution, men, women, and children in greater and greater numbers ceased to gain their living from their property and became employes instead. To them a job became the equivalent way of earning a living. At issue is whether this alteration carried with it equal or equivalent rights. A person has the right to procure his living, if he can, from the property he owns. Does he have a right to earn a living if he is an employe? If so, he has a right to his job, for that is his living.

An employer asserts his sacred right to the property he owns and uses as a means of economic gain, by undertaking operations which require the hiring of employes. He assumes that he creates the jobs. He assumes he has full right to manage his own property as he sees fit: the right to create jobs and have control of who works at those jobs: in short, the prerogative to hire and fire.

The employe, looking upon his job as his sole means of earning, believes he has an inherent right to earn a living, and therefore some inherent right in his job.

This is a deep and serious conflict, inherent in the employer-employe relationship. If the employer is right, the employe has no right to a job, which means no right to a living. If a person does not own property from which to develop income and no inherent right to earn a living in some other way, his life is drastically restricted, his liberty is drastically limited, and his pursuit of happiness is an illusion.

However political economists may argue the theories of this matter or come to theoretical conclusions, the hard practical reality of this economic insecurity of teachers--which is to say the insecurity of their jobs--is the reason good teachers are hard to find and harder to keep. School management insists that good teachers are secure because

18

they are the kind of teachers wanted. The facts do not bear this out. School management did not want Teacher Isaacs and his two friends Teachers Donald and Upton. Management wants the best teachers provided they are docile and obedient and do not incur anybody's displeasure. This is the quest for Angels.

Teachers' disastrous economic insecurity is poorly understood for several reasons. First, school management tends strongly to conservatism and generally accepts the comfortable (for management) laissez faire position regarding employment practices. Second, school management is the source of information about the schools. Teachers are not a source from which the public can become informed about their welfare and that of the pupils. The views of teachers are only individual views, for they have no means of forming a consensus.

Third, dismissal practices and rapid turnover of personnel in schools have always been so common that they are accepted as normal. Even the great majority of teachers themselves defend the status quo because teachers of inquiring minds tend to perceive their precarious economic status and depart from school work. In even greater numbers are persons with this perception who turn away from the schools without ever teaching at all.

Many teachers, employers, and self-employed persons insist stoutly either that teaching is no more insecure than other occupations, or else that job insecurity is harmless or even desirable. The usual arguments, all specious cliches, are:

1. Individual bargaining between employer and employe is equal and fair.

2. Insecurity stimulates workers to their best efforts and weeds out the weak.

3. All workers, all employers, all self-employed are alike insecure; nothing could be fairer than that teachers should share the same situation.

These stereotyped attitudes call for comment.

1. In individual bargaining, the president of Colossal Corp., Inc. has the right to hire John Doe for work on the assembly line, and John has the right to accept or reject the job if it is offered. If he chooses the latter, he has the right to seek a

job somewhere else and the President has the right to hire someone else. This thought runs smoothly by overlooking the practical point that in any case the President has no worries about where he and his family will sleep that night or where they will find food.

2. Insecurity is indeed a stimulus, but not to the pleasure and thrill of fostering learning.

3. As to insecurity in general, there are degrees of it and teachers are among workers having the highest degree.

The industrial revolution could not have come about if people in great numbers had not given up earning a living by means of their own property, to become employes. Hence, it is reasonable to argue that they should have been rewarded for this inestimable service by receiving even greater security than they had before, rather than penalized by complete loss of security. Regardless of the great benefaction they conferred on humanity, I sometimes think that in leaving their home-owned farms and shops to become employes, they must have had rocks in their heads.

A person must have reasonable security before he can plan his own future and hope to fulfill the basic functions of a normal human being, e.g., to own a home, have a family, belong to a community. Without security he is taking desperate risks to attempt such things, especially in occupations--of which teaching is one--in which the rewards accrue from continuity. All this seems to me obvious. It is certainly confirmed in my own experience.

It's no good trying to defend the insecurity of teachers by pointing out that the loss of a job in other kinds of work is sometimes not serious. Once in my youthful days as a migratory grain harvest worker I was fired by a wheat farmer because I was unable, on a day when I was not feeling well, to shock as much wheat as the young giant beside whom I was working. This was nothing. I simply got another job the next day --or perhaps it was the same day--with another wheat farmer who did not even bother to ask for references of my previous wheat shocking experience. But if I had been fired or forced to resign from my journalism teaching job twenty years later the consequences would have been serious indeed.

As this teaching job was in the largest school district of the state, my choice would have been either to seek a job in a smaller place, which probably would have damaged my pro-

20

fessional standing, or else move to another state. Either choice would have meant selling my home and breaking up all established community ties. It would have involved considerable expense of moving, which I could ill-afford, and a period of unemployment.

Some self-employed persons, such as doctors and lawyers, and the relatively few who operate small businesses without employes, believe they have a valid argument against the right-to-a-job principle because they have no such right, being dependent on their own efforts and initiative. The rejoinder to that is simple: their security is in their own hands but it would not be if they were employes. A self-employed person can fail--that is, he can lose his means of a livelihood --through incompetence or neglect. In this he is on a level with the employe. However, he can assure himself of prosperity by diligence and intelligence. The employe has no such advantage as long as administrative prerogative remains without a curb.

(Perhaps at the beginning of this discussion of job security I should have invited members of labor unions to skip it all, since they already know it by heart.)

Dismissal is a serious blow to a teacher for various reasons. It places a strain on his morale and reflects on his qualifications, making it more difficult to find another job. It usually means migrating to another community and it always involves expenditure of money and energy in becoming resettled. More serious in the long run is involuntary uprooting from a community and starting anew in another. Still more insidious and far-reaching is living year after year with the constant awareness that whether or not you actually are forcibly uprooted, you might be, through no fault of your own.

I was a teacher for 21 years and was fired only one time. That was in 1923 and the reason the management gave me was a downright and obvious falsehood. Even with this fairly good record, I knew during all of those years that I might be fired the next year and that there was absolutely nothing I could do to prevent this. In looking back now, I am more impressed than ever before with what a disastrous situation this was, and am astonished that I endured it so long. The burden of uncertainty I carried day and night for 21 years was a major detriment to everything I ever sought to accomplish. It was detrimental every single day I taught, continuously. I am certain this insecurity is detrimental to all teachers, and the worst of this is the loss to students.

For nine years I taught in one school. This appears to have been a stable situation, but that is pure illusion. All of the time during those years I knew my services might be dispensed with, come June. I knew this was still true regardless of how good a job I might be doing, how active I might be in community affairs, how well-liked I might be by my students and colleagues and the administration, how blameless my private life. It was true regardless of any consideration. This is a hell of a way to live.

Though I was not fired from this job my departure was due to the insecurity. I shall relate here how my effectiveness was vitiated by selfish forces beyond my control. I was well aware that some such mishap could befall me at any time. It finally did.

As a teacher of Journalism in this high school, I was faculty advisor for the yearbook, a student publication. Each year there was rivalry among local job printers for printing this book. Printing and engraving contracts were let each Spring for the following year. In the Spring of 1938 competition arose for the first time for the contract to make the copper engravings. I had assumed that the fair way to award contracts was to invite bids. Of all bids that met specifications, the lowest was always accepted. In case of a tie for lowest bid, it was my policy to have the student yearbook staff choose which to accept. I always supported these students in their decision.

During that 1937-'38 school year the yearbook printer was president of the school board. In the Spring his firm demanded the contract for the following year without a call for bids. I refused, and the fat was in the fire. This was enough, but it was not all. One of the two local newspapers, a locally owned morning paper, began pressing me for the engraving contract. This newspaper had never made the copper plates required for fine reproduction of photographs for yearbooks. The coarser zinc engravings were used in newspapers. I was willing to have this newspaper make the copper plates, for I had confidence in its integrity and quality.

The printer board president, however, was opposed. He was sincerely interested in the yearbook and he wanted the engraving done by the company in another city that had done it for many years, a company specializing in school yearbook engraving. His position was that the local morning paper could not do as good a job. I was caught in the middle of these cross currents of ambition and desire. I took two actions, signing a contract with the out-of-town engraving firm, with a cancellation agreement, and calling for bids for the printing.

Competition for the printing was between the board president's firm and the job printing department of the city's other newspaper, an afternoon paper not locally owned. The editor of the morning paper scolded me because this rival paper had sometimes won the bid for printing the yearbook. Thus he sought to help the board president's cause while the latter was striving to prevent his company from picking the small engraving plum.

Both were rivals of the afternoon paper, the one for job printing and the other for newspaper circulation and advertising linage. It turned out that the two yearbook printing bids were identical in amount, to the last decimal point. My students chose the board president printer, and I thereupon signed the printing contract. This did not make the officials of the afternoon paper happy. Thus this little storm brought down on me a little wrath from the afternoon paper and a great deal more from the other two firms.

But all this was only the mid-point of my troubles over this extracurricular duty; the situation shortly became deadly serious for me. When the school year ended in mid-June, the struggle over the contract for making the copper plates was not yet resolved. That summer, 1938, the owner of the morning newspaper wrote a letter to a banker member of the school board, demanding consideration of the engraving contract.

Thereupon, I was called before the board in an open meeting to explain my actions. I explained that I had always invited printing bids, in which specifications were detailed precisely, as I thought this was the fairest way to treat all local printing firms. The board members made no comment. I was certain they could not condemn me on this point, but I also knew the anger was not quelled. The board had a hot potato in its hands. I said if the board would adopt a policy on selecting a printer and engraver, I would follow it to the letter.

I explained the cancellation provision in the engraving contract I had signed. The board president was not happy with me for doing only this much at his behest to frustrate the morning paper against my own judgment and inclination. The newspaper owner's letter to the banker board member was then read. Another board member, a lawyer, scolded me for this letter.

It would have made sense, and might have been appropriate,

if I had declared my complete lack of control over letters other persons wrote to each other. It would have been proper for me then to resign. This, however, would have wrecked my teaching career and taken away my means of earning a living.

The board then adopted a policy, directing that on contracts for the yearbook, local firms should be favored whenever possible. This, of course, was no action at all. It left the status quo untouched and the onus still on my shoulders. After I left that meeting I was able, while walking home in the darkness, to indulge a wry smile at the irony of the situation, particularly that of the morning newspaper supporting the printer board president while the latter was frustrating its desires, and both were blaming me.

Yet I was in no sense gratified at being the center of attention of these local tycoons in a petty squabble over the innocent high school yearbook.

Now comes the remaining thread of the story, the crucial part for my purpose. Teachers' contracts for the next year were mailed to them on a certain date in early May. I also knew they were mailed that day, all of them but one. My contract did not arrive. In fact, at the time I was summoned to that board meeting, it was already two months overdue. I could have told the board I had nothing to do with the yearbook, as I was not then an employe of the school district.

When my contract did not arrive on time in May I waited a few days thinking this might be an oversight; but I suspected otherwise. School closed in mid-June, about a month later, and still I had no contract and no word of explanation. It may have been my misfortune that I was spending that summer at home. I remained in that city as a teacher for 13 years, during which I spent 11 summers attending 12-week sessions of graduate study. I had remained home that summer of 1938 to finish writing a book.

May and June slipped by without my knowing whether or not I had a job. July passed likewise in dead silence. Then the weeks of August started passing slowly, with foreshadowings of the opening of another school year.

This suspense ended one day late in August when my contract arrived by mail. But the dead silence continued. Neither the school board nor the superintendent nor anybody else involved spoke a single word about this incident, then or afterwards, to this day. A word from anybody would have meant something to me in that critical time and might have altered permanently my feelings about this affair.

I have been absent from that community for many years, but I have deep roots there from those years of labor there. Hundreds of my former students may be living there still, and every one of them will always be to me someone of special interest. Yet this experience will always color my feelings about that community.

During that ordeal and afterwards I was firmly resolved that I would never mention this incident as long as I was a public employe there. I also felt, however, that some day I would speak. It has been a long time.

The fact that my job was insecure is of no importance aside from my personal life. The important fact is that this is a typical situation of teachers. They have no protection from threats such as this to which I was subjected. The principal of the school was sympathetic, but he frankly told me he could do nothing in my behalf. I do not remember what the superintendent said in that board meeting. I never discussed the matter with him. Possibly he was as fatalistic as I was in the face of the predatory instincts of business for which, in the prospect of a tiny plum of profit, youngsters and teachers and educational values are irrelevant.

Chapter 4

BACKGROUND OF MIGRANCY

The awareness of migrancy was my constant company in all the days of my teaching. Inevitably it affected my every action and thought, in every direction. How could it have been otherwise? I liked teaching and hoped to continue it. But must I live all of my career not ever knowing what my situation might be next year? How often must I have to hunt for another job? Was there to be no end of my moving from one community to another?

It was burned deep in my consciousness that I must always be prepared in my mind to move next year, for there was no way of knowing when management would decree that I wasn't wanted any longer.

A teacher never knows what innocent action of his may give offense to somebody who carries influence with an administrator or board member. For the teacher there are taboos. These may not be as prevalent today as when I was teaching, though I am not sure. Some of the taboos have changed, certainly; but I do not know that they have diminished.

In some communities I knew, a teacher was wise not to be seen using tobacco; that taboo, in fact, faded and virtually disappeared during my teaching years. There were communities in which teachers were expected to attend church regularly and take an active part in church affairs. In some communities a teacher would have been cashiered for attending a dance and at least down graded for entering a theater. As to taking a sip of wine or any alcoholic beverage, a teacher might as well rob a bank or hold up a market.

I recall reading a story of American life in the 1920's in which a young woman teacher, desperate with loneliness and frustration in a small midwest community, took a calculated risk by dating one of the young men of the village, to attend a dance some miles away. On the way home afterwards, her escort attempted to rape her. She fought him off, but at the expense of torn clothing and scratched legs. She was instantly packed away from her job in disgrace; the young man was for a time a local hero, bragging openly about his exploit.

If a young man teacher had dated a girl of the community and attempted such a thing, he would have been lynched. The author of this tale paints an absolutely true picture in this story; every bit of it is true to the mores of that society and era. Our customs have since broadened greatly with regard to dating, dancing, and relations with the opposite sex, but to a much greater extent in some segments of the population than in others; and I am not sure but that other, equally repressive, taboos have arisen.

So far this discussion of the dilemmas of the migrant teacher has covered a small area. The teacher might undertake to realize the normal desires of a human being in such matters as owning a bit of property, having a family, and feeling that he belongs to a community. These would be grave risks for anyone dependent on his salary for the necessities of life. Yet, even on a teacher's relatively low salary, they would be reasonable undertakings if his job were as stable as, for instance, that of postal employes or firemen.

It was obvious to me in my teaching years that I should not allow myself to assume that I belonged in any community where I had a job. Almost without exception, people were kind and friendly. They accepted me readily enough. There was no doubt of their sincerity. I think this is easily accounted for. They simply took it for granted that teaching is a sometime occupation; that it is an occupation people follow for a few years until they are ready to settle down. The instability is institutionalized and so perpetuated.

This is disastrous for the schools. It is frustrating to a person who wants to continue teaching; for one naturally takes roots in the area where he lives. My resistance to the feeling of belonging was right, for it eased the wrench of leaving when that time came. To adapt an idea of Robert Frost's when one belongs to a community he does not have to ask anybody's permission to be there. This eliminates the teacher; he has to live not far from where he teaches but he has to have the permission of someone else to teach there. Whether he realizes it or not, he is an outsider. It is better that he know this.

People kick against the pricks of this hard reality. This is

27

understandable because it is all too human to try in every way to worm one's way around hard facts. One of the standard evasions is to say that if you want to belong in the community you can enter some other kind of work, such as taking a job in a store or bank, or becoming a salesman or maybe a lawyer. This attitude has caused me pain, and also embarrassment for the insensitivity of fellow human beings.

And of course it does not help to overcome the teacher shortage problem.

One of the festering sores of itineracy is that however attentive one may be to the need for resisting the feeling of belonging, one acquires this feeling anyway. One puts down roots willy-nilly wherever one remains for a protracted time--even a year. When one has to move, the principal cause of pain is not the uprooting, but the fact that the decision is not one's own. It is one thing to uproot voluntarily and quite another to be forced by others to give up either one's chosen community or chosen profession.

Teachers who love their work but who are discouraged by bad working conditions live under powerful pressure to resolve the dilemma by abandoning school work. One of the most powerful of these pressures is the lure of material gain by business enterprise. Teachers are constantly reminded, as we all are, that the high material rewards of our materialistic society go to business enterprise; and business experience is considered of high value for everyone.

Teacher Isaacs, with his varied talents and great energy, is undoubtedly well able to manage his affairs and support his family outside the schools. Yet he was a dedicated teacher; he had chosen to devote his talents to the propagation of learning until he was forced out by falling afoul of petty administrative machinery.

Though some readers may not have realized that the instability of the job of teaching should be a significant cause of the shortage of good teachers, the shortage itself has been a matter of concern among school people since my young days. But in all these more than fifty years I have read and heard the note of alarm and wondering regret at the schools' inability to attract and hold their share of the more promising young men and women graduates turned out annually by our colleges and universities. It has been discussed in their numerous magazines, journals, and books, and in conventions, conferences, and graduate seminars.

Curiously, however, not in any of these efforts has anyone

to my knowledge made an analysis of how the conditions under which teachers work and live affect their morale and the attractiveness of teaching as an occupation. Actually only a little analysis is necessary to establish facts of the most basic significance. The insecurity is self-evident; one need only compare job security in teaching with that in any occupation under civil service or union contract.

Here we must enlarge the scope of the discussion of bad working conditions; job insecurity is only a part. Some other aspects of personnel practices are equally as bad, and are undoubtedly more readily apprehended as offensive to decency. There are, for instance, no limitations whatever on the amount of work teachers may be required to perform, nor on hours per day or days per week they can be required to be on duty. Again, management's practices with teachers in such matters as assignments, evaluation, supervision, and accusations in dismissals are sometimes insulting and degrading, such as that of the 'drops of tea' in the accusation against Teacher Quentin. One of the most offensive and indeed unethical of established practices is abusing and harassing teachers to encourage or even force them to resign. This practice is well understood among employes anywhere, of course. Examples of its use in schools of which I shall give an account are more extreme, I think, than are found elsewhere.

Readers have seen some of this in the cases I have already presented. Other instances will be given specifically and in detail throughout the rest of the book. Countless citizens see the short hours of the school day and believe teachers have an easy job. They do not know how strenuous the teachers' hours in the classroom are nor how many non-teaching duties teachers are required to perform. There are multitudes of such duties. More will be said later about them.

At this point the entire issue in this book comes into focus: the schools lose their best teachers, the whole program of learning in the schools is fragmented and chaotic, because of rapid and incessant turnover of staffs; and morale of teachers is and has always been low because of bad working conditions.

One of these conditions I have not yet specified is the absence of any right of teachers to a voice in the conduct of their own affairs. They are completely under the domination of administration in their every act in the performance of their duties, and the manner in which they perform them. This last phrase, for instance, applies to teaching methods. It applies to the teacher's relations with her pupils. Administration has the complete prerogative either to permit a teacher to teach in accordance with methods she prefers, or to require her to abandon them entirely and conform to different practices and methods as required by administrative fiat.

It is generally agreed, I believe, that a professional has the prerogative of making decisions in the area of his competence. By this standard teachers are as far as possible from being professional. No public school teacher enjoys this prerogative. If he does make some decisions on his own it is by permission and not by right.

Well, here is a simple proposition: the conditions of employment of teachers have changed hardly an iota from what the conditions for employes were in other fields of work early in the industrial revolution. We do not have to go back that far to find vivid illustrations of conditions comparable to those of teachers today. Still living oldsters remember working conditions in fields other than teaching which would now be absolutely intolerable. In my boyhood I often heard of railroad trainmen working shifts of 16 or more hours. Many times I worked such shifts as a newspaper reporter in the 1920's, and there was no slightest thought of extra pay or compensatory time off. The next day was simply another working day. The six-day week was standard. It became also my standard to be unavailable by telephone on my day off, to avert a callback.

Before those newspaper days, as a migrant grain harvester I worked the usual normal day's shift of 13 or 14 hours, also six days a week. This was 78 to 84 hours a week. Add another 13 or 14 hours when we occasionally worked also on Sunday.

Even in the 1930's I well remember that under federal regulations the work week for some retail store employes in the city where I was then a teacher was set at 72 hours a week.

One can find records of even more drastic working conditions by harking back to the sweat shops of an earlier era, when men, women, and children spent practically all of their waking hours toiling in a condition of virtual slavery.

It seems to me hardly to be expected that employers would take the lead in ameliorating the conditions of working people.

30

How could anyone expect them to do this, when it was they who established these conditions? The many improvements for employes of later times, such as shorter hours and regular hours, safety devices, health safeguards, workman's compensation, job classifications, health and old-age pensions, extra pay for overtime, have come about mostly through labor unions and their negotiations with employers, and efforts of unions and other civic groups and individuals in securing legislation beneficial to employes.

When public school districts were formed it was natural that school boards as employers should model their practices and philosophy on those already established in private industry, and that they should assume the same prerogatives. Then as school districts grew from the one-employe to the many-employe stage, the administrator assumed the prerogatives as the board's executive officer.

Chapter 5

NO RIGHTS, NO REDRESS

An employe with no right to a job is of course in no position to secure decent working conditions. The 72-hour work week for retail store employes which was mentioned a few pages back was not negotiated by the employes; it was set under requirements of a federal law that definite working hours be established. This definite work week did not help a fatherless teenage boy whom I knew. He was employed as a clerk and general handyman in a store near where I worked. His work week, like mine, was often more than 72 hours. At about the time this federal requirement was established, this boy, then 17 years old, blew out his brains with a shotgun.

I discussed this tragic incident with the boy's employer, the proprietor of the store. He couldn't understand it; he repeated, as he had remarked to me before, that the boy had always been a good, steady worker and had never been one to complain. He was bewildered and distressed. This incident, to me, is significant to employes' working hours and other working conditions. Any employe's; even a teacher's.

Take the case of Teacher Quentin, previously mentioned. This teacher had demanded a hearing on the causes of his dismissal as a probationary teacher in a small high school. His right to such a hearing had been established by legislation enacted in 1961. I shall quote liberally from the Judge's memorandum decision.

'This case,' the Judge wrote in his decision, 'presents the distressing spectacle of an outstanding school teacher sacrificed by a small school district's Board of Trustees who were unable to stand up against the protests of parents who were overly indulgent to their children and who were also relatives, friends or important constituents of the Clerk of the Board or some other members of the Board.

32

'In 1960 the Board of _____ High requested the principal to secure a well-qualified 'tough' English teacher who would raise the level of achievement in English at _____ High. The principal secured Teacher Quentin who filled the bill precisely.'

This teacher worked long hours, helping individual students for hours after school on scores of occasions. 'His presence was a boon to the capable and ambitious students ... but a disaster to the lazy, the spoiled, and to some extent to even the average student. They had to work many hours perfecting their English, at the expense of their leisure time, their athletics and to a degree their other subjects. If they did not meet the high standard required by Teacher Quentin he had the old-fashioned habit of flunking them cold. Even though they were members of well known families in _____ or relatives of the Clerk of the Board!'

During Teacher Quentin's hearing, the Judge wrote, 'the Board listened to such inconsequential trivia as that Teacher Quentin tossed the last drops of tea from his cup on the classroom floor, that he permitted his students to read GRAPES OF WRATH (over the protests of the Clerk of the Board) and that he permitted a discussion in class of the various types of love (e.g. mother love, love of country, romantic love, sexual love, etc.). They also heard of the standards of work he demanded, his unbending requirements from his students and his lack of tact with parents.'

The Judge expressed sympathy for Teacher Quentin's contention that his dismissal should be reversed because it was wrong and an abuse of board discretion, and because his hearing was held before the same board that had given him notice of dismissal. However, the Judge pointed out that this was the kind of hearing provided by statute. He indicated his belief that the dismissal was unjust, but pointed out that the law gave him no power of redress for this kind of wrong.

He said that under the school statutes 'the court can only inquire as to whether the cause of dismissal relates solely to the welfare of the school and the pupils thereof.'

'In the present case,' the Judge wrote, 'a close reading of the transcript leaves one with the impression that the Board did not have sufficient cause to dismiss Teacher Quentin and did not have substantial evidence for its decision.'

However, the law explicitly excludes the Judge from taking this into account. He cited the passage of law on this point:

'the determination of the Board as to the sufficiency of the reasons for dismissal shall be conclusive but the cause shall relate solely to the welfare of the school and the pupils thereof...' And 'No right of judicial review shall exist for such employe on the question of the sufficiency of the reasons for the dismissal.'

The Judge said, in short, that the reasons were not sufficient, but he had no authority to correct this injustice.

One further statement the Judge made in this case must be noted. Referring to the 1961 legislation granting probationary teachers the right of a hearing on dismissal, he said, 'These rights granted the probationary teacher may seem slight and illusory, but before 1961 he had no rights whatsoever. (Emphasis added.) He could be dismissed at the end of the school year for any or no cause and had no redress.' (Emphasis added.)

This is an extraordinarily sweeping and unqualified statement. It is obviously true and it has been true since the founding of the public schools. I do not know how many citizens are aware of it and I think there are few who realize its far-reaching implications. Before 1961 the California probationary teacher had no rights whatsoever. Since then he has had the 'slight and illusory' right of judicial review of the question whether the cause of his dismissal relates solely to the welfare of the school and its pupils. The Judge took due note that the cause did not need to be supported with substantial evidence. This Judge might have said the same regarding the cause of firing Teacher Isaacs. Also of multitudes of other fired teachers.

None can dispute the Judge's words 'no rights whatsoever' and 'no redress.' They are true facts. They have been demonstrated countless times through the whole history of public education in the United States. I doubt that one can find a school district in this nation which has not at some time dismissed a teacher for any or no cause and with no redress.

Here is the basic point of this book. Here is the whole case.

From these facts it follows that bad working conditions and bad personnel practices have developed and flourished and become institutionalized and finally accepted as the normal and proper order of things in the schools. All of the rights and all of the redress are on the side of the teacher's employer. He can make whatever disposition he chooses of the teachers. He can say to one come, and he cometh; to another go, and he goeth.

He can say, and did say, to Teacher Hazel Kelly in the middle of the school year that next week another teacher would take her third grade class and she would move to another school to a fifth grade class. More than 40 years ago he said to Dwight Mitchell, whose major field of study was English, and who later wrote this book, 'You will teach biology, bookkeeping, and general science, and you will coach athletics and conduct the school orchestra.' And this was done--after a fashion.

No teacher, however successful and experienced, has any right whatsoever to use the method he has found successful, to establish relations with his pupils and deal with them in ways that are natural to him and that build the best rapport; to plan his teaching program in his own way, in ways he has proved by experience. He is subject at all times to the dictates of management in all of his acts and the manner in which he performs them.

This unquestioned authority, become traditional by long usage, partly explains the casual, often even careless attitude of school management toward teachers and the often flimsy reasons given for dismissing them. If my use here of the term management is confusing, it means the school board and administration. This manner of dismissing, and also certain tactics used to encourage teachers to resign and to discourage them from resisting dismissal are further explained by two other considerations. One, the need of administrators to secure their own positions, has been mentioned. The other is an outcome of two conflicting philosophies of the proper relations between administration and teachers.

One philosophy or theory is simply that of business management toward employes, that management has carte blanche prerogative to dispose of employes at will, with no obligation to explain anything. The other is that all school workers involved in the educational process are colleagues or fellow workers, all on some vague basis of equality. Some administrators subscribe to one of these theories, some to the other; and some, apparently, try to take a middle course, or subscribe to both at once, or to switch from one to the other as the situation may seem to make advantageous.

The colleagues theory has the prestige of long tradition, from early days when there actually was a shortage of persons with sufficient education to qualify for teaching. The solution was to appoint the best qualified as Principal Teacher. His job was not only to carry his full share of teaching but also to supervise and train the others in an endeavor to raise their qualifications to a satisfactory level. Eventually the word 'Teacher' was dropped from the title; but the tradition of equal colleagues has persisted. Incidentally, when the Principal Teacher's time became all engrossed in administering, other persons took over the duties of supervising teachers.

The colleague theory is fortified, too, by the tradition that since one of the most important functions of the schools is to teach democracy, pure and undefiled, the schools must practice democracy among their own personnel.

This means full and free discussion, full and free clash of conflicting opinions and philosophies of education. So much for abstract theory. What it means in the heat of actual conflict of ideas and interests is another matter. Administration, as it observes the dissenters in the conflict of ideas, does not lose sight of its prerogative to control jobs, and also to influence the further destinies of employes who are fired. Certain practices which have developed in this situation are of prime concern for us here. We have observed some of them in the dismissal of Teachers Isaacs and Quentin. The practice of giving reasons for dismissal may seem to some readers to have been corrupted in the Teachers Isaacs and Quentin dismissals. They force one to doubt that the reasons given were sufficient, and then, save the mark, to question whether they were the real reasons. There was no doubt at all in the Judge's mind that in the dismissal of Teacher Quentin the reasons were insufficient; indeed that the teacher was 'sacrificed.'

Both of these cases were actually typical and nothing more, out of many that have come to my attention. I think the cases can be explained rather simply: administrators are themselves insecure, they must beware of employes who may be a threat to them by gaining community prestige, they must pay heed to the 'democratic' tradition, and the reasons they give for dismissal have been traditionally accepted as sufficient evidence; therefore they are quite careless about the reasons they give.

Back of this is the preparation they make for justifying dismissals. They build a case against a teacher before making the dismissal step. We must give considerable attention to certain common practices in this preparation.

We are not concerned here with dismissal of teachers

whose performance is obviously unsatisfactory and not to the best interest of the young learners, but with dismissals for reasons of questionable validity, such as those given for firing Teachers Isaacs and Quentin.

The building of a case against a teacher often impels her to resign. This is gratifying to her employers, saving them the unpleasant job of telling her she is dismissed. It also avoids the unpleasantness, and sometimes danger to them, of publicity. The administration's preparations therefore include tactics known among practically all employers and employes, of making the employe's job unpleasant. There are so many well-known ways to do this that it seems unnecessary to give details here.

More than ten years ago a school principal acquaintance of mine whom I here call Administrator Grant Iverson--since I am not identifying individuals in this book--related some practices of building a case against a teacher. The administrator, he said, observes the teacher without her knowledge, for instance as she is supervising the playground. He notes the time of her arrival at school in the morning and after lunch. He gathers information about her wherever he can. He makes note of any infractions of rules, of any actions, or information that can be construed against the teacher. He writes this in full and is careful to date it. These notes he keeps, perhaps placing them in the teacher's personnel file, which is considered confidential; if the teacher demands to see her file the administrator if he wishes can remove material from it before allowing her to open it.

The administrator makes note of any complaints he receives about the teacher. He may tell her he has received such complaints and threaten her with them, without informing her of any particulars such as the identity of the complainers.

For instance when Teacher Freda George was fired after administrative harassment one of her alleged disqualifications was that someone was alleged to have said she ate potato chips in the classroom. No evidence was taken from anybody claiming to have seen this heinous offense. This practice of basing complaints on unidentified or faceless accusers is one I have encountered again and again; so often indeed that when aggrieved teachers have started to tell me their experiences in being fired I have assumed that the faceless accusers tactic was used. Some of them have thereupon asked in surprise how I learned about their cases.

I was once told, years after the occasion, that I had been

downgraded because someone said I smoked while teaching in the classroom. In all my years of teaching, this is something I never did. One of the evils of nurturing damaging reports from unidentified sources is that it encourages others to fabricate, spread, and magnify rumors and false reports. Falstaff, that immortal comic character of Shakespeare's, commenting on his physical corpulence and mental agility, said, 'I am not only witty in myself, but the cause that wit is in other men.' The purveyor of slander might paraphrase this, 'I am not only slanderous in myself but the cause that slander is in other men.'

Chapter 6

TECHNIQUES OF THE TREATMENT

This administrative harassing of teachers has been a long established practice in various school districts. A careful observer of the practice soon becomes familiar with the tactics used, such as unidentified informers, or faceless accusers. All teachers, and citizens generally, also should be aware of them. Therefore the more common types of them are sketched in this chapter.

In the mid-1950's I was relating an instance of such a harassment case to a man who had extensive knowledge of its use against teachers, including himself. His summarizing comment, 'That's the same old pattern,' puzzled me then. Not long afterward another friend of mine, also a teacher and a deeply humane man of wisdom and experience, referred to these tactics as 'The Treatment.'

This apparently cynical talk from two such men shocked me. As a teacher I had had a few unpleasant experiences with administration myself, but I had not yet become aware of the full scope of this harassing practice. Circumstances then put me in a position in which I could not help becoming aware of it; I found it on every hand. My friends, I then came to realize, had not been cynical at all; they were only objective and resolute in the face of a hostile condition.

The two terms I learned from them have clung to me and become a part of my vocabulary on the subject. As instance after instance of the dismissal practices has come to my attention I have learned to recognize the pattern of them. The term 'The Treatment' is an apt one for the tactics. It is my name for them.

Some faceless accusers are only casual or incidental, as particular occasions arise. In large organizations, however

39

and in small ones more or less, administrators have regular informers, generally among their employes. These lackeys ply a trade known of old, of course, and without honor. Theirs is a dubious route to advancement. Yet in the schools some innocent teachers, timid and trusting, are flattered by the attention of an administrator and easily beguiled into giving desired information. Their reward is often contemptuous dismissal when their usefulness to the administration is ended. I have known some of these victims.

Among other tactics of The Treatment, I have already menttioned the use of secret personnel files. One of the reasons given for keeping them secret is that disclosure of sources of confidential information is a violation of professional ethics. These secret dossiers are not as prominent as they were ten years ago. They seem to have fallen into disrepute as controversy over teacher dismissals has been publicized occasionally, making the public aware of their unethical character and uses. Also most of the secrecy has been found to be of questionable legality, as I shall explain later.

Confuse, divide, and conquer: these three words identify widely known tactics of long and effective use. They are partticularly valuable to a new administration, which is always concerned about employes who owe their jobs and sometimes their loyalties to the previous administration.

Often in school districts that have had a stable administration for years there are some cohesive groups of teachers such as the teaching staffs of individual schools. Principals know the value of such staffs with whom they have had good rapport. A new superintendent is wary of such groups and often breaks them up by transferring many teachers to other schools, breaking the potential threat of collective solidarity. This action also serves another purpose; it encourages the principals and teachers to seek greener pastures, either in another school district, or often, in some occupation other than school work.

I observed a completely successful instance of this in 1962 and 1963. Two principals whom I am calling Administrators Hugh Everett and Loren Inverness saw their prized teaching staffs scattered after a change of district administration, and both of them resigned. One left the public schools entirely and the other found a non-administrative school position. Their departure was of course an important part of the victory for which the new superintendent was striving. Many teachers resigned, some were dismissed. I mention such in-

40

stances because even though occurrences of this nature are common, specific cases bring the reality of the matter more sharply to awareness than is possible with the merely general and abstract.

Scattering of teaching staffs creates confusion to the new superintendent's advantage. Other means to the same end are easily available. I have observed administrators, in speaking to individuals and groups, hint of anonymous sources of information that some employes have been making unwarrented criticism of the administration or the Board of Trustees or the school program. They insist that such talk is unethical and must stop. By concealing the identity of the offenders, offenses, and source of information, the administrator casts a shadow of suspicion over all. His hearers are silenced and suspicious, and some perhaps roused to eagerness for sensation.

Employes with spirit and enterprise--that is, the best employes--will turn their thoughts to greener pastures, thus furthering the administration's purpose, while intensifying the shortage of teachers.

In 1966 I heard the new administrator of a college use a tactic closely resembling this in an address to an alumni group. He made some mildly complimentary remarks about the faculty, but pointedly added that he did not mean to include all of its members. Thus he cast suspicion and doubt against and among faculty members generally. Some could not help wondering whether they were on the administrator's disapproved list, and who else was on it. Unless this kind of scattergun slander is challenged, the harm it causes may continue for years.

I have mentioned administrators spying on teachers. Since the machinery of administration includes a good many rules and procedures, everyone occasionally inadvertently violates some rule. The administration may thereupon punish selectively, as Teacher Isaacs was punished. More recently Teacher Clara Ingalls has been forced out of her tenure position on accusation of violating a minor rule which few teachers avoid violating occasionally.

Thus this was also a case of selective punishment, raising doubt as to the district management's real motive in getting rid of her. The fact that this was a new administration seeking to become established lends force to the honest doubt.

A simple method of spying is to observe teachers during a

41

discussion such as a faculty meeting, or a mixed group of schoolmen and lay citizens. Often when such a group meets with an interest in some matter the administration does not want to be concerned with and may even oppose, the members have an incentive to talk freely and are encouraged to do so, with the assurance that of course the utmost democracy prevails.

Eventually the members of the group will exhaust the subject and themselves and the group will fade away leaving the participants the pleasant feeling of having got something off their chests and having produced a report which elicits a pat on the back from the Board of Trustees and which haply nobody will ever read. The administrator meanwhile will have taken the measure of all of them and determined which dissenters among the teachers may be a threat to him. He will know how to deal with them afterwards.

This is no more true democracy than if a slave holder of Ante Bellum had said to his slaves, 'Speak your minds freely. Say anything you want to say. And take the consequences.'

Teacher Russell Roberts related to me a clumsy substitute of the spying tactic. His principal stood inside the school entrance in the mornings with his watch in his hand. If any teacher entered after the prescribed time, he pointed an accusing finger at her and dramatically exclaimed 'You're late!' This betrayed a lack of finesse. The principal did not hold this job long; but long enough to demoralize the teaching staff and cause several teachers to resign. Teacher Roberts left the public schools and has never returned.

Administrators bent on building a case against a teacher can gather information with utmost ease that they can construe to the teacher's disfavor. For instance a quick look into a classroom gives a basis for saying the room was disorderly or too orderly, or that a spelling or arithmetic lesson was not exactly on schedule as prescribed by the lockstep course of study or the teacher's own required written lesson plans. The administrator may note how a teacher reacts when he finds a new lock on his classroom door without his having been notified or given the key. Opportunities for such covert harassment are endless.

Some information on these practices was given me by Administrator Iverson who had protested mildly after having been made to serve for a year as the hatchet man of his superintendent, Administrator Anton Downs, who was engaged for several years in eliminating the old teaching staff of his

42

district. Administrator Iverson was dismissed, of course, shortly afterward. The record of his protest followed him and he had to resort to substitute teaching for a year to support his family before he was able, with great difficulty, to rehabilitate himself in school work in a distant part of the State.

Teachers struggling to survive harassment sometimes find themselves handicapped by the schoolmen's Code of Professional Ethics. It requires that personnel matters, such as grievances and dismissals, be resolved among school people only. Dirty linen should not be washed in public. The code provides channels of appeal for an aggrieved person to progressively higher authorities. The first step is to approach the other party to the dispute. If this fails, a teacher appeals to her principal. (He of course may be the other party.) Failing redress here, the teacher goes to the next higher authority, who may be the superintendent or one of his deputies; finally, to the Board of Trustees.

The associations of school persons, all units or affiliates of the National Education Association, provide further appeals; there may be an ethics committee of the aggrieved teacher's associates in her own district. From there she could appeal to ethics officials of larger association units such as a regional or state association.

In my observation this system has fatal flaws and the reasons are not hard to find. In all serious grievances the teacher's job is at stake, and perhaps also her career. As management's prerogative of control of jobs is never questioned, the teacher's only basis of appeal is to mercy or to ideal justice. If the ethics officials deem the teacher worthy, they may help her find a job in another district.

With all its power, administration dominates the association and all of its subdivisions and affiliates. Members of the district's ethics committee are just as vulnerable to administrative power as the aggrieved teacher. Such a committee can deliver only what its administration wants. As the ethics code forbids involving persons outside the professional family, the teacher is ultimately left standing absolutely alone.

Teacher Carmen Thomas summarized this entire case. She wrote to me, 'They tell you to take your grievances to the higher-ups; when you do. they all line up against you.'

Early French fur trappers of the Hudson's Bay Co. explored the Clearwater River area in what is now the State of Idaho not long after the Lewis and Clark party paddled their canoes down that stream in 1805 on their historic journey of exploration to the Pacific Ocean. Going up one of the small tributaries, a group of these trappers found themselves in a canyon which suddenly terminated in impassible rock walls.

Their phrase for such a place, cul de sac, survives today in a village of that area named Culdesac. To me there is a parallel in this with the grievance system for teachers. The so-called channels of appeal for the teacher are not channels but cul de sacs. There is no appeal to disinterested adjudication. The teacher is still in an individual bargaining situation and the powers all line up against her.

The tactics of discrimination against an unwanted person are familiar to nearly all employes. Teachers are particularly vulnerable for a number of reasons, including the lack of cohesion among them and the fact that their work makes heavy demands on unselfish devotion to the young, a requirement tending to inhibit them from developing tough defensive armor.

Techniques of making a teacher's situation unpleasant, that is of harassing her, are on every hand: for example changing without due notice such regulations as hours a teacher is required to be at school; making difficult deadlines and changing deadlines without sufficient notice and with vague explanations, for various reports required of teachers--daily, weekly, monthly, annual, etc.; making mountains of molehills such as minor errors in reports; questioning whether pupils have been justly graded; ignoring or being dilatory with a teacher's orders or requests for books and other necessary supplies; requiring excessive non-teaching work such as most of the above, and also including extra-curricular duties such as sponsoring student clubs and activities, and attending PTA and faculty and committee meetings. The possibilities are endless.

Teachers are theoretically exempt, more or less, from certain supposedly menial jobs such as janitor work and hoeing thistles and puncture weeds out of the playgrounds. This rudimentary degree of job classification may not apply in one-room school districts where it would be impracticable, and it is easily evaded elsewhere. Teacher Thomas complained that she had to do most of the janitor work in her classroom. The school janitor, she said, only swept the floor. She did all the rest, such as wiping the desks and other furniture,

44

the blackboards, and windows.

'My work,' she said, 'is 50 per cent clerical, 25 per cent janitorial and 25 per cent teaching.'

This system, she said, enabled the school district to economize on janitors. It would be unjust to censure the janitors without further inquiry. They may have been overworked. If the janitor was negligent and/or arrogant, this could indicate that the administration paid more deference to him than to the teachers. This is not said facetiously. I taught in more than one school in which the janitor's salary was higher than that of the teachers. Nor was it politic of a teacher to offer suggestions for janitorial improvement.

That was long ago; but not nearly as long ago Teacher Russell Roberts wrote me what he had learned: 'One morning I arrived a bit earlier than usual and the janitor was still cleaning up my room. To my horror he used the same mop to dust the tops of the desks that he used on the floor! When I politely questioned his method he told me to 'stick to teachin'. I'll clean up as I please!' When I brought the matter up to my superior he told me never to get on the bad side of the janitor. After this the janitor left my room strictly alone. The first class in the morning and I had to clean up.'

Sometimes a crucial part of the dismissal of a teacher is a conference or several conferences between her and one or more administrators. In the State in which I live probationary teachers, that is, teachers not on tenure, have been automatically rehired on May 15 each year unless they were formally notified of dismissal. The notices may be by mail but usually the teacher is informed beforehand. This conference can be trying for the administrator as well as a nightmare for the teacher, especially if she is sensitive or inclined to resist. In the latter case a conference may serve the aim of overcoming resistance.

One instance of this was Teacher Hazel Kelly's afternoon conference of four and a half hours with three administrators. She was a tenure teacher who, being unintimidated, was under long-term harassment. In another case, I was in Teacher Edith Frank's school on business at a time when administrators were taking turns conferring-- or 'conferencing' to employ a term used by the educators--with her, one after the other. Teacher Freda George informed me orally of some of her 'conferencing' and I have a copy of Teacher Ralph Gilbert's written account of some of his experiences in conference. In none of these did they gain headway by individual bargaining.

For another tactic of The Treatment I have used the term sapping. I have known some school management men to undermine a teacher while appearing to be doing something else. One technique is to be solicitous to the teacher or her friends about her health. Another is to question her closely about her work, the appearance of her classroom, the progress of some of her pupils; this questioning may be on minute details. Subtle shades of manner and tone of voice in response to mention of a teacher can be effective. Even the interpretation of results of standardized tests of a teacher's class can be construed unfavorably for the teacher.

I close this discussion of The Treatment with mention of a tactic I call Hostages and Reprisals. One can easily enough find parents who shrink from criticizing the schools or defending a teacher beleaguered by The Treatment for fear of reprisal against their children. I have found this fear widespread among parents. I cannot account for it if there is no ground for it. This is a dreadful blot on our schools and our society.

Chapter 7

BREAKING TENURE: INITIAL STEPS

A person seriously concerned about economic occupational
security is often balked by stereotyped attitudes over simpli-
fied to the point that they make little sense.

E. g.: 1. The commercial free enterprise stereotype: insecurity is the only good state because it makes us hustle. 2.
The-world-owes-us-a-living stereotype; security is a God-
given right, to save us from discouragement. 3. A typical
school administrative stereotype: give teachers job security
and they become drones forthwith. 4. A widespread view of
the unthinking: security is either absolute or non-existent. 5.
Another of the same ilk: security is bad for adventurers;
therefore it is bad for teachers, salesmen, scholars, everybody.

Once in a discussion of the plight of teachers an intelligent
business acquaintance of mine lapsed into an irrelevant business stereotype which has the air of settling the question of
economic security once and for all: 'I've never had a secure
job in my life and I don't want one.'

Many citizens, perhaps from these contradictory stereotypes in their cultural heritage, believe that tenure assures
proper security for teachers. This is error, for three reason: first, of all persons who ever accept teaching positions,
few attain tenure; second, a teacher loses tenure by transferring to another district; third, and far the most basic,
tenure teachers are under the same administrative domination and working conditions as the probationary teachers.

The administration can carry to the Board of Trustees the
same kinds of complaints against tenure teachers that were
made against Teachers Isaacs and Quentin, without having to
provide substantive evidence. It has a completely free hand
in assigning them teaching and non-teaching duties and di-

47

recting them in every detail of their work. It can require of them more work than is humanly possible to perform. It can get rid of them by these and other mistreatments. The established security of a tenure teacher is the right of a court hearing in case of dismissal; but there is no redress if the school management forces such a teacher to resign by setting up impossible working conditions.

I give here an account of one instance in which this was done.

This teacher had actually been secure for many years, teaching in a small school district which was rare because it was committed to the belief that the young actually want to learn, and the problem therefore is to give them full scope to this innate desire. In the words of the then superintendent, Administrator Manuel Peters, 'Learning must be exact and as wide and deep as possible. But more than this, it must be in an atmosphere that is desirable and pleasurable, and lead to the habit (his emphasis) of wanting to learn.'

Supported by this rare enlightened philosophy, Teacher Kelly taught for many years with outstanding success, and with growing devotion and enthusiasm in helping the young find ways of releasing their innate desire to learn. Another of the stereotypes of our culture is the opposite, that the young detest learning and can be brought to it only through coercion, conniving, and sheer force, indeed through beating and fear. This is totally erroneous.

Youngsters cannot help wanting to learn, for they live in a world with older persons to whom they look for guidance and help in all things; and these older ones know multitudes of things and have power in many things beyond the capacity of the young. Inevitably youngsters yearn to attain and surpass these abilities.

Under Administrator Peters' regime of almost two decades this small elementary school became known far and wide. Its graduates were outstanding as they advanced into secondary and higher education. Its many visitors were amazed at the high performance of the students and their superb morale. This school was the special pride and show place of a large school of education on a nearby university campus.

Such devotion as that of Teacher Kelly is not at all unusual among the nation's public school teachers. There are many thousands of such teachers who do not need insecurity as a spur. There would be more if bad working conditions were

48

corrected.

After World War II a rapid influx of new residents brought about a change in the temper of this community. Many of the newcomers were disturbed because the school did not fit the conventional stereotype of a school. Missing were the traditional herding of youngsters into and out of classrooms in some precise order prescribed from an administrative office; the lockstep daily schedule of classes; the corporal punishments; the rigid division of each class into three groups; various other regimentations.

Superintendent Peters retired.

Here was a challenging situation for an ambitious successor, to establish a small empire for himself, in the process weeding out, of course, the enlightened program of learning and the teachers devoted to it. He would face delicate problems, for there still are many older residents who appreciate the famed success of Administrator Peters during nearly two decades. There are parents who have had the deep satisfaction of seeing their offspring develop gloriously the habit of wanting to learn. Many of these residents had chosen to live in this community because of the rare opportunity the school afforded their sons and daughters.

Administrator Anton Downs was elected superintendent in the Spring of 1951. There was hope among the teachers that he would continue the policies that had made the small community a noteworthy center of enthusiastic learning. Dissention among district citizens still being high, there was strong opposition to this appointment. Malcontents who feared that this man would follow the model of Superintendent Peters organized to exert pressure for his ouster.

Teacher Kelly, seeking to counter this reactionary move, gave a letter to the trustees stating that if Superintendent Downs were dismissed, she would resign in protest. However, Downs survived this storm. Under the precarious conditions, he trod a wary path during his first year, making no noteworthy move against the district's traditional teaching methods. On one occasion he gave a hint of strong arm potential. In the middle of his first year the new vice-principal--the district's first--was ousted after conviction of a morals offense. When this incident was aired in the press, Downs called a faculty meeting and laid down the law to the teachers: they were not to speak of the incident to anyone;

49

'You may say that Mr ‑‑‑‑‑‑‑‑‑ is not here any more, and that is all you may say.'

The spectacle of an administrator rising thus above the First Amendment to the Constitution of the United States is not rare. It is not rare in the schools, and its occurrence not infrequently separates the submissive teachers from those of free mind and spirit, who depart for other fields of endeavor. It gave Teacher Kelly a sudden and jarring insight into the character of the man in whose behalf less than a year before she had laid her own career in the balance.

It is simple discretion that the new broom of the superintendent's office be used with a delicate touch before it starts sweeping clean. In the fall of 1952 the administrative proliferation in this small one-school district surged a little further, with a full ranking principal under the superintendent, in place of the ill-starred vice-principal of Administrator Downs' first year. It now became the principal's chore to be the superintendent's right hand man in demolishing the old staff and the old teaching practices. This is often part of a minor administrator's apprenticeship for a hoped-for superintendency himself. He must prove himself in practicing the tactics of The Treatment.

Teacher Kelly did not realize when in the Fall of 1952 she began receiving notes from the Principal, Administrator Elmer Lyons, that this was the beginning of a campaign which would end with her having to choose between abandoning her job or her teaching methods of proved superiority. She saw the principal's actions as only an instance of unpleasant behavior on the part of one of her fellow employes. She was then still a typical teacher in her unawareness of established school administrative practices of harassing. Four years later, when this particular school administration had finished with her, she understood all too well how a new school management secures its position by sweeping away potential dissent. She learned the techniques used and she was sadder and wiser.

Teacher Kelly received a letter dated Oct. 15, 1952 from Administrator Lyons containing so much revealing material that I shall present a good deal of it here. It opens: 'This is to confirm my oral statement to you this morning concerning your practice of often referring to children directly by their last name. As I explained to you in our conversation, you are asked in the future to refer to children directly by using their first names. All teachers in _____ (school) will be expected to follow this practice.'

Perhaps it is apparent, in the context of this prolixity, that Principal Lyons' phrase 'referring to pupils directly' must mean 'addressing pupils.' Teacher Kelly had indeed been in the habit of addressing them by their last names, and for cause; this evoked a mature response. It established good teacher-pupil rapport. Some years after this I visited a metal shop class for seventh grade boys on the first day of the semester. The teacher at first addressed these pupils as 'boys,' but presently he occasionally said 'men' as if he were addressing a crew of men on a job. Before the end of that first class session he completely dropped the word 'boys'; the students were men.

He was evoking a mature response. This was important.

We are involved here with an important and unfortunately widely misunderstood principle, the innate responsiveness of human beings. No human relationship fostering growth of the spirit can be harnessed with rigid rules and thou-shalt-nots. I can imagine some administrative ass reprimanding that shop teacher for addressing those boys as 'men.'

Personal relationship between teacher and pupil is just about as crucial as anything can be in learning. Unfortunately school officialdom presents a united front against teacher opposition to stupid acts of its members, such as Administrator Lyons' stricture against the technique Teacher Kelly had used for years with fruitful results. This closing of ranks seems required as 'professional ethics.'

The experience of two high school teachers is an example. Teacher Delbert Brown demanded of his pupils their best efforts at all times. He was a hard taskmaster who inspired enthusiasm and a potent loyalty in his students, along with their kicking against the pricks of his unrelenting pressure.

One of his more brilliant students, a girl with a flair for the melodramatic, once wrote for him an essay on the general futility of living. It was a bravura piece with tongue-in-cheek, with which this intelligent teenager tested the teacher's credulity, probably knowing he would see her effort for what it was. He did. He read through all her pseudo reasons for finding nothing worth while in life, and as one of his comments he scribbled in the margin, 'Have you tried suicide?'

This was good for a chuckle among the girl and her friends when he returned the paper to her; but it became an issue when the administration decided to fire this teacher. It was contended that he had done a dastardly deed, putting the idea

51

of suicide in the mind of the pupil. There was a public hearing, a crowd of more than 200 citizens was emotionally stirred, in pro- and contra- camps. A psychiatrist witness condemned the teacher's comment, the educational hierarchy closed ranks, and Teacher Brown had to make two trips across the continent to find another job 3,000 miles away.

He was more lucky than his friend and colleague Teacher Joel Conway, who had the temerity to speak a few words in support of his colleague Brown. He too was fired, and he found that no other school superintendent in his State would hire him. I discussed this case with Administrator Claudia Xavier of another school district, who held a Ph. D. degree in psychology. She took her stand in the closed ranks.

I had asked her somewhat playfully if this pother over the 'suicide' comment wasn't rather absurd. She answered seriously that never under any circumstance would she approve anyone's saying such a thing as that to anybody.

This was in accord with what the psychiatrist had said at the hearing. Well, this dictum seems to bar all banter. You must not say playfully to anyone 'go to hell'; for the person might take you seriously, and go.

Back to Administrator Lyons' letter. He wrote, 'Any parent making a complaint against a teacher directly to this office, will be instructed to discuss the matter with the teacher involved.' He said if this step fails to secure peace, the parent has the recourse of appealing to the Principal, 'and from the Principal, if necessary, to the Superintendent, and finally to the Board of Trustees, whose decision becomes final.'

This statement equates the operation of procedural machinery with justice. It assumes that either the matter will be resolved to satisfaction somewhere along the way, or else that in the decision of the trustees, which is final, all losses are restored and sorrows end. Persons who have pondered the deep problem of justice know that though clearly defined procedures are essential, procedure is a perverted instrument when used not as a means to justice, but as an end in itself. The latter is mere play-acting, like the Teacher Isaacs hearing.

Second, Principal Lyons' stated policy of having complaining parents talk with teachers complained about was proper; but a policy may sometimes spring into existence on the instant and back out again in the same manner. For some three years from the time this letter was written, Teacher Kelly heard not just a few times but many about alleged parents' complaints, although not more than three or four of these parents ever materialized in flesh and blood before her. This instant policy seems repeatedly to have slipped in and out again.

During those years the complaining parents gambit was a numbers game played by Administrator Downs and his passing procession of principals, at the average rate of one new principal a year. Sometimes the word was that one-third of the parents were complaining, sometimes two-thirds, sometimes a half. In one of my conversations with Downs the number was a precise 23.

Teacher Kelly always welcomed visitors to her classroom. Once for several weeks parents came in pairs or groups, relaying one group in the mornings and another in the afternoons. They did not indicate what their grievances were, if any; they did not even complain. They did not state why they were there.

In after years one of these parents confessed to Teacher Kelly that her conscience had troubled her for her part in this mysterious visiting game. To Teacher Kelly's disappointment she did not state why her conscience had suffered this flare-up. For some persons partial confession seems to lessen the burden so that they prefer to tolerate the reduced weight of conscience rather than to tell all.

Now for one more item in the letter of Administrator Lyons. He named one of the alleged complaining parents and said she 'quoted you (i.e. Teacher Kelly) as making the following statement, which if true, is in my opinion a serious thing:

"I did not get the arithmetic book I wanted, so I will not teach it.'

'I hope you did not make such a statement, (sic) however since you have been quoted as saying this, I wish to call your attention to the following facts.'

Hereupon he cited his 'facts'; the State Education Code and district board policy required that this particular book be used. I believe that this school administrator, this Doctor of Education, could understand that the teacher would not 'teach' the book if she did not have it. He was practicing harassment, though awkwardly.

53

He also said the arithmetic book 'is available in you room.' Perhaps it was when he wrote the letter. It was not there when Teacher Kelly made the statement--if she made it. It was awkward of Administrator Lyons to ignore the facts in what he put in writing. After this the cause of learning in his school could hardly be advanced through his relation with this teacher. What he did accomplish was to compound confusion and antagonism and make confidence and trust impossible. He must have known this; but it was irrelevant. Administration is important; learning is incidental. In short he practiced the standard tactics of The Treatment.

His intentions appear more clearly in his next letter to Teacher Kelly dated Nov. 12, 1952, just four weeks after the previous one. It dealt with an alleged conference between him and Teacher Kelly which was actually an impromptu conversation while she was supervising the playground. They discussed the matter of alleged complaining parents.

This letter opens with, 'In looking over the notes I jotted down after our conference Tuesday, I note that we discussed the below named topics and made the following plans concerning them. . . . '

The letter thereupon launched into several items which, according to Teacher Kelly, they had not talked about at all; and it did not mention the one matter they had talked about, the complaining parents. It recited a number of items which 'we agreed' on and 'we decided'; on more time for social studies; use of the state arithmetic textbook; on how many pupils should be allowed to 'leave the room' during class sessions instead of using recess time for their personal needs.

This letter compounded the confusion. Lyons had previously refused to supply certain arithmetic material Teacher Kelly had requested. Now he said 'If you decide upon supplementary arithmetic materials that you would like to use, let me know about it and I'll try to arrange to secure them for you.' This almost seems to be an instant policy change, but vagueness saves it from that.

Vagueness can also be achieved by faulty grammar, as in 'According to your daily schedule, you had allowed thirty minutes a day for four days be lengthened to about fifty minutes.' And, 'We discussed many things not mentioned above, (sic) however, these seem to me to be the most important ones.' Perhaps these solecisms are unintentional; I am not informed as to English requirements in the Doctor of Education program.

Chapter 8

BREAKING TENURE: TIGHTENING THE VISE

Here we recall briefly the elaborate machinery of administration. We have been dealing with a teacher's problem with her principal. Both are cogs in the administrative machine. The movement of cogs and pistons and pulleys in a machine is not an isolated affair but an integral part of the movement of the entire machine. Principal Lyons' small forays against Teacher Kelly could not have been isolated incidents involving just him and her; the chains of command in the school administrative machine are clear, especially in a small school district of only one elementary school and not more than twenty teachers.

Superintendent Downs, then in his second year in this district, had employed Principal Lyons. Inevitably, Lyons was fully aware of the policies it was his duty to execute. One of the processes of winnowing fledgling principals for possible advancement is to put to the test their stamina in being the new broom that sweeps clean; i. e., in clearing away obstacles to the security of the new regime; i.e., in 'not rehiring' employes (teachers) who might feel some nostalgia for the preceding regime; i. e., in blasting the careers and livelihood of fellow school workers out of tender solicitude for the comfort and security of the new superintendent and his regime-in-the-making.

I have mentioned the ceremonies attendant upon the separation of teachers from their jobs. These ceremonies may include written evaluations by the principal and other administrators after actual or ostensible visitations to the classroom of the victim; perhaps written self-evaluations by the employe; conferences. If the teacher is determined to fight dismissal he may make the dreary round of appeals to the 'higher ups.'

None of these rituals will save the teacher's job and they will impair his chances of finding another. Yet if the teacher has the temperament to enjoy all of the attention he receives in this going through channels he may derive some satisfaction in pursuing them to the end. However, if the appealing employe is merely interested in justice, in ascertaining the true reasons for dismissal or in reversing the dismissal action, especially if he knows he has been doing a good job, then all the trapesing through the procedural channels is likely to be a bitterly disheartening experience.

If the teacher appeals to regional or state or national educational associations of the school hierarchy, his frustrations will mount accordingly. As Teacher Carmen Thomas said, 'They all line up against you.'

All this is by way of indicating that although it was the principal who wrote the letters to Teacher Kelly, he was not acting independently. The purport of the letters was a matter of policy laid down for him. This point must be clear in all of the discussion of Teacher Kelly and her tenure job; for though the principal administered much of The Treatment, the authority and responsibility rest with the superintendent. The principal may have been inept at times but he knew the policy he was expected to follow.

Teacher Kelly's introduction to The Treatment in 1952 was followed by a lull but not a cessation for a little more than two years. Among occasional reminders that the administrative purpose toward her was only quasi-dormant was the illegal detention of her sixth grade daughter in the classroom during recess for several days without explanation.

After these several days of reprisal against an involuntary hostage during which, the daughter said, Teacher Royce Atkins remained silent except for occasional tapping of his pencil on his desk, one day he blurted out a question, asking the girl why she had spread gossip through the neighborhood about the resignation of Teacher Fannie Zink from the district while the school year was in progress. She was shocked, being unaware of any gossip about this teacher's departure.

Teacher Kelly supposed that this treatment was merely unaccountable ignorant arrogance on the part of her colleague Teacher Atkins. It was not until later that she became fully aware of the pattern of harassment, after she had been subjected to the full gamut of it.

She regretted afterward, as did I, that she did not take prompt and vigorous action, including legal action if necessary. Had she done this successfully the school district administration would have suffered nothing but the unfavorable publicity. The onus would have fallen on Teacher Atkins, and this would have been partial justice. He would have been the scapegoat, but the root of the matter would have been untouched; for knowing persons would perceive at once that Teacher Atkins was only selling his soul to carry out orders. All that was a decade and more ago but the conditions have not changed. I am aware at this moment, June 15, 1966, of several cases now in progress that would serve my purpose as well as this one. None of the material in this book is out of date; not even my being fired from a high school in 1923 on a pretext that was patently a bare-faced lie. There has never been a significant change in the basic power structure and practices of the public schools relative to the status of teachers.

During the two years in which Teacher Kelly was spared all but incidental harassment after the first onslaught there was a 75 per cent turnover of the teaching staff. The new broom had plenty of sweeping to do and had done a great deal of it. On June 30, 1954 ten of the teachers separated from the district that spring petitioned the Board of Trustees to ask the State Teachers' Association to investigate administrative practices of the district 'for the past three years.'

Note that these teachers did not address their petition directly to the association. They were careful to go through channels. I have known the association to refuse aggrieved teachers' pleas for help, on the ground that the teachers' employers did not concur in the request. Fortunately in law enforcement a man who has been robbed can obtain the aid of police without the consent of the robber.

The teachers said in their petition: 'We feel this action is necessary for the good of the school; to protect teachers within the district, to promote more professional and inspired teaching, and to attract applicants of the highest caliber.'

Nothing came of this petition.

These ten teachers obviously did not leave the district willingly, unless willingness had been induced by the new regime. They were more than half of the total teaching staff. The new broom had swept vigorously.

Shortly before this petition Administrator Downs wrote a

letter dated April 28, 1954 to one of Teacher Kelly's colleagues, here called Teacher Teresa Underwood, which contains a number of statements relevant to the lowly status of teachers. It refers to Teacher Underwood's dismissal by that year's principal, Administrator Grant Iverson, and 'my (Superintendent Downs) intention to concur.' The superintendent's letter states that this dismissal was in accordance with board policy, inasmuch as 'It is his (Principal Iverson's) opinion,. . . . that you should not be offered a contract for 1954-55.'

This is the administrative prerogative in the concrete and the specific, and stated explicitly. Perhaps a specific example such as this of the casual wrecking of one person's career may lend more poignant meaning than mere awarness of the prerogative in the abstract, widespread as this awareness is. Teacher Underwood left the public schools permanently.

The superintendent next said in his letter, 'This opinion was arrived at independently and it was not his (Principal Iverson's) intention at any time to give the impression that he was speaking for anyone other than himself.' This statement could have served the superintendent another purpose, namely that if trouble should arise from this action of the principal's the onus would fall on him and the superintendent would escape blame. The letter was a weapon against both the teacher and the principal. Principals as well as teachers are expendable on occasion. This principal was very soon expended. It was he who had to be a substitute teacher for a year while he was laboring to rehabilitate himself.

Teacher Underwood and Principal Iverson may typify The American School Employe, anywhere across the land--beside fragrant pine woods of Maine, in lush Iowa when corn sprouts of Spring push up in the furrows, in a crowded street of Philadelphia or brawling Chicago, in the mile-high air of Colorado, in the tobacco and cotton fields of Dixie, or beside the sluggish San Joaquin river of the great California valley. They were The American School Employe finding out by experience the meaning of management prerogative.

As the two went away from school in the sudden deep loneliness of disfavor, thousands of teachers across the land were also finding themselves lonely discards. If they had known about each other in their common plight they might have communicated with and consoled each other.

The superintendent did, however, volunteer a statement of

his own to Teacher Underwood regarding his concurrence: 'I feel that the present situation is in no way a reflection on your effectiveness in the classroom, but rather is an outgrowth of your not being able to relinquish the role of a parent-citizen and assume that of a member of the teaching staff.'

Yet this same administrator if questioned would certainly have declared vehemently his utter devotion to democracy. His statement suggests adding a clause to a teacher's contract such as this: 'In accepting this position I relinquish my citizenship and parenthood.'

Readers must have recognized irony in my phrase 'turning democracy on and off at will.' Would it matter much if Superintendent Downs turned it off only long enough to dictate to his secretary one little sentence of only 46 words? It matters a great deal to persons who look upon democracy as something more than a game.

Not long after his spring housecleaning of personnel I remarked to Administrator Downs that it seemed to me his job was fraught with difficulties. He answered that this was so at times but that he had been having a lot of fun. Yet there was no law requiring the district management to give Teacher Underwood any explanation for her dismissal. Possibly the administration protested too much.

The case was different for Teacher Kelly, for she had tenure, and Teacher Underwood did not. This meant that Teacher Kelly had the right, in the event of dismissal, to a public hearing and an appeal to court, requiring management to present substantial evidence of valid cause for dismissal. A court case is often embarrassing to the school management. It is also very hazardous to the teacher. Even if the court sustains her she will have incurred the displeasure of the 'higher-ups' in education.

Teacher Kelly had assumed despite Principal Lyons' letters, the illegal detention of her daughter, and other annoyances, that her tenure made her safe from any serious attack on the continuance of her teaching career. She was disturbed but not unduly worried even when she received a copy of a letter concerning her written March 4, 1955 by Administrator Downs to the then principal, Administrator Glenn Young, the successor to Principal Lyons. (There was an average of one principal a year during those years.) We now turn to this letter, which was a definite intimation that something new was pending which would not be trivial.

59

The superintendent said that for the past several weeks a number of parents had complained to him about Teacher Kelly's classroom program and that 'similar situations' had arisen annually for four years; that he had always urged these parents to visit Teacher Kelly's class and confer with her; that they had a right to confer with the principal. 'I believe,' he wrote, 'that it is our responsibility to determine whether or not there is any basis for such criticism and if so, take steps to correct it.'

This was two and a half years after Principal Lyons had enunciated the policy under which he 'directed' aggrieved parents to confer with the teacher involved; and of course instant policy could have changed often during that time. Now the policy was merely to urge classroom visits and conferring. The superintendent knew that Teacher Kelly had taught in that district for 12 years and had been greatly admired by colleagues and parents. He could have told her what these parents' complaints were. He could have visited her classroom himself and observed her excellent teaching. Simple, honest steps such as these would be taken for granted in other fields of employment.

But this was The Treatment. In actuality no parents did confer with the teacher. In other walks of life conferring over a grievance is taken for granted. It is inescapable that either there were no complaining parents, or else they were a strange lot, or somebody influenced them not to confer. There was a period of some weeks at about the time of this March 4, 1955 letter during which mothers came by relays in teams and sat in Teacher Kelly's classroom for hours. If they had grievances they were strangely tongue-tied.

The crucial part of this letter by the superintendent was that there should be a meeting of the parents of Teacher Kelly's pupils, at which she would be required to defend her teaching program. He wrote: 'We have a responsibility to protect teachers from unjustified pressures and criticisms. However, we also have responsibilities to students and parents. I believe that the above plan offers the best possibility for relieving a situation unpleasant for all of us.'

Teacher Kelly considered this proposal carefully and rejected it as unwise and unethical. A mass meeting on issues of which she had been kept in the dark, with unidentified persons who could not or would not speak openly and frankly, would be a dangerously explosive situation. Where civil conduct had been conspicuously missing, civil restraint could not be expected. The only prospect was for evil consequences to herself and the other participants, possibly developing into a district-wide disturbance. She chose to do all possible to prevent the harm such an outcome would bring to the district's youngsters.

Teacher Kelly always welcomed visitors to her classroom. She believed implicitly that citizens have a right to make such visits; for the schools are public just as roads and city parks are public and the people have right of access to public property and to know what is happening there. She welcomed the teams and relays of women and they accepted her hospitality without ever giving her an inkling of their purpose. She knows nothing of it to this day. Nor has she ever had any certain information as to whether the superintendent knew of these visitations or whether the visitors were some of the parents who he said in his letter had complained to him and whom he said he had urged to talk with her.

Adminstrator Downs' proposal brings us back to the old typical school management concept of adjudication for a teacher, that accusation unsupported with evidence is proof and let the teacher fend for himself as best he can. Teacher Kelly was to be required to perform instant magic in refuting charges about which she knew nothing. Teachers Isaacs and Quentin had to fend for themselves. It is not hard to find as many other examples as one could want.

This proposed meeting was abandoned when Teacher Kelly's attorney--a woman who donated her services--elicited from the school management the admission they could not legally force it upon her. Thereupon management quickly took advantage of an alternative. The district had scheduled an open house on the night of March 10, just six days after Administrator Downs' letter. Parents were invited to spend the evening at the school, with each teacher in her classroom as hostess to all visitors.

The time and energy teachers had to spend preparing for this affair might better have been expended in teaching; but let that pass; open house is only one of a multitude of school affairs that take precedence over the mere matter of helping youngsters to learn and develop a love of learning.

This normally gala affair turned out to bear some resemblance to the proposed meeting with disgruntled parents which Administrator Downs had proposed. One woman visitor appeared to be dissatisfied about something. I attended that open house and could determine only that she was disgruntled with something about Teacher Kelly. When someone pointed out to her some of the good work of her daughter on display, she declared she was not interested in that but in what the whole class had been doing. (This was also on display.) Presently she began questioning Teacher Kelly about her educational theories and practices. An embarrassed silence fell on the room. Teacher Kelly suggested to this woman that she write her questions.

Then to relieve the tension Teacher Kelly started a program of entertainment she had planned. While a violinist was playing Fritz Kreisler's 'Liebesfreud,' Principal Young continued an unbroken buzz of conversation with a woman sitting beside him. The violinist said afterwards that this was the only time he had ever used his violin as a combat weapon.

A moment after this violin solo with accompaniment of piano and two speaking voices, Administrator Downs appeared at the door. Principal Young's facial expression seemed to convey a message to him and he vanished without entering the room. Soon after, the open house, thus turned dismal despite the teacher's elaborate preparation, and dissonant with the unrehearsed oral accompaniment of the solo, ended in general silence.

Nine days later Administrator Downs ordered Teacher Kelly by letter to appear before the Board of Trustees in executive session on March 23. She had no hint, from the letter or elsewhere, of the business to be transacted. She assumed it would not be trivial, or pleasant. She was right. In this meeting the school management played its ace in this game of breaking a tenure teacher. Teacher Kelly learned there that she had been accused, tried, and found guilty, and sentenced, all without her knowledge. The board president, Trustee Percy Frederick, then handed her a letter stating the case, all complete, even to the written penalty.

She was told thus that she had been found incompetent; it was the 'opinion' or 'judgment' of her principal that she had not been teaching the minimums required by the courses of study. Her alleged deficiencies were not specified; and of course no evidence was cited to support the accusations; and the abundant evidence to the contrary that lay on every hand was conveniently ignored.

There was evidence for instance that for more than a decade Teacher Kelly's pupils had consistently developed a love of learning under her tutelage, had consistently recorded high

62

scores in achievement tests, and had demonstrated year after year the thoroughness of her teaching by succeeding in later years of schooling.

As always in such cases the judgment was considered final; hence there was no occasion for delay in administering the penalty. This is labor-saving adjudication: instant accusation which is also instant evidence; instant judgment, instant sentencing. For some strange reason the courts appear not interested in this marvellously simple and easy way to administer infallible justice.

Chapter 9

BREAKING TENURE: THE 21-HOUR WORK DAY

Teacher Kelly's punishment was a requirement that she prepare minutely detailed daily lesson plans requiring many hours of work each day, in eight subjects: reading, arithmetic, language arts, spelling, science, social studies, health, and music. This punishment was applied at the discretion of the administrators and they took full advantage of this power.

Principal Young outlined their demands in a lengthy letter to the teacher, giving extensive and minute directions for preparation of the lesson plans. The blank forms Teacher Kelly was required to make and fill out required two typed pages each day for each lesson plan. To save herself the labor of copying these blanks she mimeographed them by the hundreds, at her own expense and on her own time. She had to fill ten of these forms each day, as three of them were required in reading, one for each of the three groups into which the class was divided, and one for each of the seven other subjects. Thus she had to fill blank spaces in a total of twenty pages of outline forms each day.

(The division of a class into three groups on the basis of mental capacity or achievement as determined by objective tests has been a categorically absolute requirement in many schools in recent years.)

Administrative neglect to enforce the standard triune segregation--high, average, and low ability--in the seven other subjects was never explained. The opportunity existed, presumably, to force this teacher to make three separate plans for each of the eight subjects. This would have made 48 pages a day. The total remained, however, at 20 pages.

Conditions of teachers' lives have changed since the 1870's. There is a tradition--or maybe it is an actual record--of rules a school principal is said to have laid down for his teachers in 1872. One of the rules was: 'After ten hours in school, the teacher may spend the remaining time reading the Bible or some other good books.'

Teacher Kelly did not spend her 'remaining time' reading the Bible; she spent it making lesson plans. In checking these forms, I counted the number of words the teacher had to write for a typical day's lesson plan assignment. There were seven items of a routine nature: three places for the date, two for the teacher's name, and two for the subject title. There are 12 blank spaces in each plan for the teacher to use in writing the plans themselves. This makes 19 spaces to be filled in each plan, or 190 for the ten plans.

On one 20-page set of plans I counted 140 routine words written in, and 620 words describing the day's plans, for a total of 760 words Teacher Kelly wrote in the plans for that day. The two-page outlines have 320 mimeographed words, or 3,200 in the ten outlines of one day. Thus the total was 3,960 words in each set of daily plans.

These figures do not touch the formidable basic task at all, that of preparing the plans before writing them. This included framing a statement of the day's objectives in terms acceptable to the administration, which had the absolute prerogative of rejecting and demanding anything according to preference or fancy; describing the content of each lesson each day; listing materials to be used; describing teaching procedures; and, oddly, writing an evaluation of the results. This was odd because the teacher was required to give her plans to the principal two days before she was to use them. They were never returned to her. The management did not explain how to evaluate the results beforehand.

Although I once had to prepare some make-believe plans during my teacher training days, I have sought the opinions of experienced elementary teachers as to how much of a burden Teacher Kelly's lesson plan assignment was. One teacher said an experienced person might be able to produce the 20 pages of plans in a day if she could give it her full time, but certainly not while teaching.

I asked a number of elementary teachers this question: Under average normal conditions, what would be a reasonable time an experienced teacher would require to make a plan for one lesson in one subject for one day, using this two-page form? One of these teachers answered that working with care and thoroughness to write a plan as nearly perfect as possible, one would require a full day. On the other extreme, another teacher said she believed she could make a plan that would be acceptable under ordinary circumstances in 20 minutes. No other teacher estimated less than an hour; most estimates were for an hour or hour and a half.

These teachers did not know my reasons for seeking their opinions. All are intelligent, successful teachers who have proved themselves by years of experience. I accept their estimates as fair and authoritative. Thus this assignment to Teacher Kelly was a job of 10 to 15 hours a day. In the lowest estimate of 20 minutes for a plan, the assignment amounts to 200 minutes, or three hours and 20 minutes of hard, intensive work each day. And for what? For the teacher to state what she intended to do each day, how she would go about it, what she hoped to accomplish, and, in the realm of the miraculous, what she thought beforehand she had accomplished.

I have carbon copies of many of these actual plans; they can be seen, touched, smelled and read.

I attribute to most readers the capacity of being shocked by this. Suppose we compromise between the 10 hours and 15 hours for lesson plans, assuming they were a 12-hour job. Teacher Kelly was busy in school eight hours a day. She had other duties, clerical work, attending meetings, making trips to libraries, conferring with parents, etc. Allow that on an average this required an hour a day, a very conservative estimate.

With all this we have a 21-hour work day assigned to this teacher by these administrators dedicated to helping youngsters learn. Again, I credit to readers the capacity of seeing this as shocking. I have discussed this with a good many school administrators, and some of them were shocked; but I found none ready to take a stand openly against it. I see cause for deep concern in the indifference, or at least inertia, of responsible persons, school and lay citizens alike, in the face, not just of this incident, but the conditions that make possible and invite the subjection of teachers to such indignities as this.

Persons in other occupations have defenses against such treatment. For teachers there is no defense whatsoever, as the judge in Teacher Quentin's hearing noted. While this persecution of Teacher Kelly was in progress I discussed it with a schoolman I am calling Administrator Norris Zander who I

The following four pages present a reproduction of one-tenth of Teacher Kelly's lesson plan assignment for one day.

Date ___June 9, 1955___   Subject ___Social Studies___

OUTLINE GUIDE FOR DAILY PLAN

Teacher Kil

One assumption upon which teaching is based is that <u>thorough planning</u> <u>will make for better teaching</u>. The planning includes both <u>long-range plans</u> <u>and daily plans</u>.

Prior to <u>making detailed plans</u>, the teacher will have learned what the general class situation is. Information as to the kind of <u>community</u>, the school policies, the programs of study, the <u>course objectives</u>, materials <u>yet to be taught</u>, plus relevant <u>information on the students in the class</u>—— all these will provide a background vital to effective planning.

I. Objectives

    a. Desired pupil "outcomes": Understandings or generalizations; skills or abilities; attitudes; interests, or habits.
        Social studies instruction is particularly committed to the preservation and extension of the democratic way of life, and to the development of the highest type of democratic behavior on the part of each child.

    b. With relation to broader objectives stated in the long-range plans.
        Skills to achieve while working together: taking turns, sharing ideas and materials, getting other person's points of view, giving and receiving

II. Content criticisms objectively, planning and evaluating work, arranging exhibits,

working on committees, taking responsibility for part of a job, and doing
a separate section of the daily plan, or see IV. An outline of one's share.
concepts or information essential to development of desired generaliza-
tions and other objectives. Outline may be topical statements or major
questions and sub-questions which reflect the day's objectives. Include
sufficient details to be meaningful to and usable by the teacher.

America a Good Place to Live

Free Education for All
Churches in America
Life, Liberty, and the Pursuit of Happiness
We Fight for Freedom

A Second World War
The United Nations
Keep America a Good Place to
Live.

III. Materials

    a. Necessary materials for learning activities during the class period.

        1. Books   "America's Own Story" Beversaux
                    "My Country", Ames, Ames, Cusley

        2. Audio-visual Aids Making charts on "Things That Make Our Country a Good
                        Place to Live." Pictures showing some rights of "life,
                        liberty, and the pursuit of happiness."

        3. Tools, etc.   Work of the United Nations (articles from newspapers.)

IV. Procedure

    a. Three phases of activities, showing what teacher and pupils will
       do in carrying out desired learning activities.

Date __June 9, 1955__   Subject __Social Studies__

1. Introductory Activities

    a. The <u>approach</u>: "Setting the Stage" for further
        learning, motivation, orientation.

        Children that were interested in the subject <u>Churches</u>
        <u>in America</u> will report information that they have
        gathered from outside sources. Discuss; early colonial
        churches, pioneer churches, frontier village churches.
        Difficulty in obtaining preachers. What did they mean

2. Developmental Activities by Camp Meetings?

    a. The <u>body</u> of the class period: the lesson proper,
        outgrowth of 1-a, major phase of activities

        Talk about the influence of the church in towns. How
        do churches help people to live better lives? Bring
        about thinking of honesty, truthful, loyalty to God
        and to country. Remark on the importance of the

3. Culminating Activities Declaration of Independence. This
                    was to begin the fight for freedom

    a. The climax of the class session: A tying-together in
        of the learning experiences and a looking- America.
        forward to future class activities. (Includes
        any or all: Summarization, Review, Evaluation,
        Assignment, Planning for further pupil activi-
        ties.) Children will look up the Declaration of
        Independence and read the part that indicates that all

ren have the right to "life, liberty, and the pursuit of happiness." Who guarantees this rights? Do all countries have these rights? Encourage children to read story page 344 "America's Own Story? Plan to continue on this subject at the next social studies period. Children should try to define life, liberty, and the pursuit of happiness.

V. Teacher's Self-Evaluation

A. To develop further competency jot down answers to:

1. How successful was the class session? What went well? What needs improvement?

   a. What went well? What needs improvement?

      (1) Adequacy of planning

      (2) Appropriateness of objectives, content, materials, and procedures.

2. What changes should be made in order to improve this plan?

_____

Teacher Kelly

thought because of his position might exert some pressure in behalf of Teacher Kelly. After more than an hour of fruitless talk, I suggested that no teacher could possibly carry out this lesson plan assignment. His reply and parting shot was 'She can try.' This disheartened me, but it definitely contributed to my enlightenment.

A superintendent friend of mine, a humane man, once remarked to me that the greatest problem of school administrators is the worst ones among them. Should he read this I am glad to say to him and his fellows, 'My friend, and gentlemen, Adminstrator Downs by way of example.'

Teacher Kelly did manage to supply the administration with the lesson plans, as ordered. Her pupils continued to learn with high spirit and morale until the end of the year. I do not know whether the management was aware of that.

She also had other matters to attend to. Following the lesson plan punishment there was a flurry of letters and memos demanding answers, of meetings (sometimes in educational jargon called 'conferencing'), and responding to office notices; all of which might have a comic opera flavor for one not close enough to the scene to feel the deadly seriousness of a human career at stake.

One of these distractions from teaching turned on Teacher Kelly's sacrilege in not making proper obeisance to the current educational fashion of dividing the class into three 'ability' groups, upper, middle, and lower. The flying squadrons of supervisors, testers, etc. rushed in to rescue her from this heresy. After due 'conferencing' they decided to administer objective tests to her pupils to determine their placement in the three groups.

Unfortunately for beautiful theory, the test results placed two-thirds of the pupils in the top group and all the rest except one lone boy in the middle group. The pedagogic pundits were caught in a dilemma. To make a regrouping would discredit the infallible scientific tests. They chose the lesser evil of insisting on the lopsided grouping the tests decreed. This required solemn conclaves on how to handle such a big group as the top one, and how to fill out a daily two-page lesson plan for the low 'group' of just one boy.

Apparently omitted from consideration was the delicate possibility that Teacher Kelly's excellent instruction might have something to do with the pupils' remarkably high achievement record. The painstaking efforts to demonstrate

72

her incompetence would have been better supported if the tests had shown two-thirds on the bottom and only one pupil at the top.

This teacher stood in critical need of friends and she found that she did not lack friends. Many individuals, teachers and lay citizens alike, spoke in her defense. They protested, orally and in writing, to the trustees and Administration. They attempted to reason with them; they secured a substantial number of signatures of district residents to a petition in her behalf.

These loyal and devoted efforts could not save her job. Individual and sporadic group efforts in such a situation are futile against solidly entrenched organization. They are as futile as the efforts of a bank clerk trying to reason with a robber who is pointing a gun at him.

Teacher Kelly appealed as a dues paying member to the State Teachers' association. Her plight was also made known to a considerable number of administrators of varying degrees of influence in the state association. Two high ranking officials of the association each spent several hours listening intently to the details of her problem. One offered to mediate, but only on condition Teacher Kelly ignore all that had happened and endeavor to secure herself in the superintendent's regard. She could not accept this of course, for she knew past acts cannot trammel up their consequences. The other official made no comment and took no action. All of Teacher Kelly's search for help from the organization men and women was, like my experience with Administrator Zander, disheartening but enlightening. They could never help of course as long as management's every wish is sacred to them.

Teacher Kelly did find an organization of teachers who had perfect understanding and who gave her unstinting help in every way they could. This was the American Federation of Teachers. It was a small group. It was unable to secure justice or even save her job or her professional standing. It did, however, provide abundantly what any person most needs in a time of tribulation, counsel and understanding, staunch friendship, and moral support. She cast her lot permanently with this group.

The school management persistently demanded that Teacher Kelly accumulate more credits in teacher training courses. Such study is regarded as the sovereign road to improvement, as it is indeed the road to a higher salary. It also helps to swell enrollment in the teacher training schools. Teacher Kelly saw possible entrapment in this direction, but no possibility of an acceptable or honorable settlement of the issue. She had studied God's plenty of teacher training courses; but she was a master teacher and she knew that any school of education would close ranks with her antagonists; for, to quote Teacher Carmen Thomas again, 'they all line up against you.'

One technique of The Treatment is to bombard the teacher with questions and demand immediate answers. Teacher Kelly received this treatment from a group of the 'higher ups' assembled with Administrator Downs in his office. It was a remarkable occasion. He handed her a list of 35 questions-- not counting sub-headings under some of them-- in a conference of four hours and thirteen minutes starting at 1:06 p.m. and ending at 5:19 p.m. He demanded that she answer them on the spot. She did so in her own way, writing each question and her answer to it, one at a time, and reading them the answer. Her 21 pages of this handwriting are still in her possession, along with the copy of the 35-plus questions.

During this happy afternoon's 'conferencing'--and it was a hot late Spring day--the other persons present occasionally excused themselves one at a time. None suggested that she, too, might need to excuse herself for personal reasons, being also human, and a Migrant but not an Angel. When she finally extended herself the courtesy of an excuse, the response from them was a grunt. It may be argued I suppose that this scanting of the amenities was an example of laudable diligence in concentrating on the purpose at hand.

In the Fall of 1955 Teacher Kelly was denied a classroom. She and her friends thereupon felt that a test case in court to determine whether or not a tenured teacher has a right to a class would be an important contribution to public education. So indeed it might have been. It would also have placed Teacher Kelly in greater jeopardy of her teaching career and would have involved expenses not easy to meet. She postponed the issue by asking for and receiving a year's leave of absence. This was in late September.

In the Spring of 1956 a so-called Ethics Council of her fellow teachers issued a statement signed by two of them suggesting that 'she should have followed one of the following three courses:

'1. Followed the recommendations of the Board of Trustees.

74

'2. Used democratic group processes within the _____ District Teachers' Association to arrive at an acceptable solution.

'3. Sought employment in a district where her philosophy and that of the district were more in accord.'

This council urged that 'When she returns from her leave of absence, one of the above courses of action should be pursued.'

This ethics group evidently failed to perceive that upon her 'return' she could hardly pursue that third course. However unpopular it may be to criticize anyone's written expression, it is nonetheless pertinent and sometimes needful to point out the solecisms in linguistic communication, whether by these Ethics Council members or by Administrator Lyons, are evidences of slovenly thought.

During part of Teacher Kelly's leave she taught in another school district, in which her ability to encourage in her pupils the growth of the habit of desiring to learn and to meet and solve their personal conflicts and problems was recognized and appreciated. The superintendent believed teachers should have freedom to function at maximum efficiency according to their individual traits and abilities. He fully accepted teachers, pupils, and people generally as fellow human beings. I wondered how long this man would remain in school administration. It wasn't much longer.

At the end of the year's leave, Teacher Kelly faced again the question of taking legal action; it was of doubtful issue; it was a grave peril to her means of earning a living; funds for a court fight were not in sight. The mere problem of physical stamina to carry a full-time job and a full-time fight at the same time was formidable--to say nothing of the 10 to 15 hours a day writing lesson plans, and undergoing any other punishment the management might devise at will.

In any case if she should return to the district where she had taught 12 years and in which she had tenure, she would not be allowed to teach. The superintendent had assured her that he had other duties for her to perform--at his discretion. She was thus deprived of her profession, and nothing was sure. Ladies and Gentlemen, what would you have done? She resigned.

Chapter 10

HIGHER EDUCATION: FEAR AT THE TOP

In my pre-university late teens I heard about a controversial English professor in the university of a sparsely-populated State where I hoped to take a degree. A few years later I found myself enrolled, to my trepidation, in his class in Elizabethan Drama. I expected to encounter an ogre; for the shocking reports I had heard about him were that he had challenged his students to think critically about established mores and customs of the age, and that he was divorced.

To my surprise this professor was not a huge, overbearing vaunting rebel but a middle-aged, physically small, mild mannered, and serious man. I had problems in that class but they were not what I had expected. The professor made no onslaughts on my cherished middle class beliefs. My grades reflected his quick apprehension of my poor preparation for upper division study. I knew this was just. Yet he never belittled me in any way and he spoke to me kindly enough whenever I met him on the campus or street.

A year of two later I learned that this man was no longer on the faculty. After that he distinguished himself by scholarly writing but I believe he did not teach any more. I never knew whether he was dismissed or whether he simply found the narrow mindedness intolerable. His departure, I have always believed, gratified some powerful forces in the state.

This lack of certainty disqualifies the case of this professor as an example of outright cashiering of a competent, humane teacher. For this, however, it is all the more worthy of a brief mention, for reasons that are more basic if less obvious than if he had been fired. My mind was poisoned against this professor by the malign talk before my university years merely from my being a resident of that state, though I had not seen that campus. Ergo, the minds of a good many other youngsters must have been similarly tainted by the same bigotry. It is not possible that I could have been the only youth who heard the malicious talk.

I am sure that this was a specific instance in which the cause of learning, which is the cause of humanity, suffered by the evil tongue of intolerance and prejudice. Of course there are countless other such instances. A careful, steady look at just one, like this, illuminates the whole evil process. I am one of many whose enlightenment of mind and spirit was damaged and retarded by unjust derogation of this man, when justice and truth would have been served by words of opposite import, objective and generous recognition of his excellence as a man and teacher.

This all happened more than 40 years ago and that professor has been dead many years. I do not know whether the university administration defended him. Perhaps so, for administration was closer then to teachers, I believe, than it is now. The plight of teachers has not improved, as I think two more recent cases will show, one of the 1950's, the other of the 1960's.

Teachers in higher education in the United States suffer many of the unsatisfactory working conditions that plague public school teachers, even though their condition appears to be somewhat more stable in practice. This is by tradition rather than from recognition of any rights to which these employes might be entitled; such rights, for instance, as might be established in the Constitution or by law or contract.

The system of supervision that prevails in public schools, especially elementary schools, is absent. College and university administration is not cluttered to the same degree as in lower educational levels with task forces such as vice-principals and coordinators to regulate in detail the teachers' classroom activities and methods.

Nevertheless administrative power to make teachers toe the line is much the same at all levels, as is, at least to some degree, the practice of accepting accusation unsupported by evidence. Pressures of public bigotry and selfish interest inspire caution and fear in administration in higher education as in elementary and secondary schools. Administration cashiered Teacher Vergil Jasper for example, before public pressure started, avowedly to forestall it. The college president, Administrator Hugh Everett, was perhaps correct in expecting public pressure. Even so, he himself made this case a public issue by bringing it before the Board of Directors of the college in a regular public meeting. Schools usually do their utmost to prevent personnel difficulties from reaching the ears of outsiders. School management and the organizations which it dominates dread unfavorable publicity and make every effort to settle disputes internally. They invoke so-called professional ethics to prevent their members from making outsiders privy to their disputes.

The dispute over Teacher Jasper in the winter of 1964-'65 arose from his leadership of a college sponsored poetry reading group in which students, faculty members, and townspeople participated.

My information about this case is from what I accept as an unimpeachable source, a printed report of an American Civil Liberties Union investigation of the affair. My copy of the report was placed in my hands by a person who saved it for me. We were then more than a thousand miles from the college. I have seen the picturesque college campus, set on an irregular hill, forested and rocky, with a grand spectacle around it of peaks of the Shining Mountains, dense forests, and rugged desert.

Another instance of harassing a university professor, Samuel Darrell, appears to have started from a purely internal mixup without involvement of students or the public. They became involved later. Continuing for many years, it eventually came to the attention of the press. Professor Darrell was an exceptionally successful professor of Journalism, so much so that the publicity was augmented by vigorous protests of numerous alumni when they learned that he had been driven from the classroom.

The fact that teachers in higher education are subjected to The Treatment just as teachers are in lower grade levels indicates the similarity of working conditions, as well as personnel practices. Reasons for this similarity are not hard to find. One is the dominance of administration, not only in schools and universities, but generally in our entire economy. The rise of this dominance has meant a change in the character of administrators in schools of all levels of learning. In an earlier day school executives were traditionally men of learning, of scholarly bent. Predominantly those of today are simply administrators, much like their counterparts in business and industry. In an occupational classification of workers they are of the class of administrators and not at any level of teachers. University professors and elementary teachers are occupationally closer to each other than administrators are to either.

Another force widening and deepening the separation of administrators and teachers is the teacher training institutions. It is in the schools and departments of education that the theories and philosophies of school administration are developed and promulgated. It is in these institutions that the theory was developed and became dominant that school administrators are business managers. These institutions produce the public school administrators as well as the teachers. Many of their professors are former administrators. Many college and university administrators, including presidents, are products of schools of education and schools of physical education.

For these and other reasons there are links between the public schools and higher educational institutions in their management practices which go far to make the security problem of teachers much alike at all levels. The plight of Teachers Darrell and Jasper was one with that of public school teachers I have mentioned, such as Isaacs, Kelly, and Quentin.

Administrator Everett had appointed Teacher Jasper leader of the new 'Parnassus' literary society. The program of this society included listening to readings and taped recordings of poetry, and discussions of poetry. Intimations of trouble appeared almost immediately. According to the report of the American Civil Liberties Union, which investigated the case at Jasper's request, the administration strongly objected to Jasper's selections of poetry. One of Everett's assistants, Administrator Raymond Lund, declared the programs to be in poor taste.

Thereupon Jasper arranged a program of panel discussions of what constitutes poor taste and obscenity. After this discussion the group accepted a suggestion by Jasper of hearing a tape recording of Allen Ginsberg's poem HOWL. He explained that this poem contains words widely considered objectionable. He mentioned one of them, a four-letter word through long tradition regarded as obscene.

Administrator Everett thereupon issued a warning in which he referred to administrative fear of public pressure. 'I pointed out,' he wrote later in a report of the case, 'that . . . if the work conducted by the Society was offensive to the majority of the body politic, which I indicated to be the entire constituency of the college district, pressures could be brought to bear upon the administration of this school to dissolve the Society. I further indicated that in a democracy a public institution is bound by the will of the majority of the people who support us.'

To me it is not surprising that administration feared public censorship of literary readings, particularly contemporary poetry. Maybe the danger of public outcry was greater in a sparsely populated area such as the district of this college than in a metropolitan area, though I am not sure. I have no information whether this danger was taken into account before the Parnassus literary project was launched. Such forethought might be taken for granted. Yet a faculty sponsor would rebel, if he were a person of integrity, against infringment of academic freedom. A truly free discussion will not boggle merely if it happens to involve three classes of words regarded by many--and different words in different ages--as in poor taste or obscene: words of profanity, elimination of body wastes, and sex. In our age the list has narrowed to little more than a small list of words relating to sex. Even in Queen Victoria's time W. S. Gilbert managed very well with a discreet 'damn' in one of his librettos.

I have an edition of Byron, undated but of Victoria's time. Byron's greatest work, 'Don Juan,' is bowdlerized to short selections totaling one-eighth of the entire work. Few persons today would be shocked by the remaining seven-eighths. Obscenity is whatever is offensive to the mind and spirit, never entirely the same to any two different persons. Is a person obscene to mention some happening which he considers obscene? Many of the incidents I am relating in this book are obscene to me.

A few weeks later, on Jan. 6, 1965, Teacher Jasper announced the HOWL tape would be heard in the Jan. 11 night meeting. In the afternoon of that day the College Executive Council, in a special meeting called by the College President, Administrator Everett, recommended that if the HOWL tape were heard, the President should suspend college sponsorship of the group. Teacher Jasper was not informed of either this meeting or recommendation.

Some faculty and administration members, including Administrator Lund, a dean, attended the society meeting that night and heard the recording, but raised no objection to it and did not try to prevent students from attending. It was two days later, on Jan. 13, that President Everett made the matter public by reporting it to the College Directors. The next day he informed Teacher Jasper he would not be reemployed, and suggested he resign. Two days later Jasper protested in a letter to the President that this action restricted his rights to free expression. Everett then promptly ordered dissolution of the Society.

Jasper refused to recognize this action and publicly announced the Society would meet on January 18 in his home and that the HOWL tape would be played again. The President ordered him to desist from his activities with the Society 'or any other activities of this general nature.' The Jan. 18 meeting was the last one for the society. Four days later Jasper resigned as its leader. During the controversy the administration intimated that Teacher Jasper did not have harmonious relations with other faculty members.

The A. C. L. U.'s judgments on this case confirm the insecurity, indeed helplessness, of teachers to protect themselves from attack from any quarter--administration, Directors, or public. President Everett assumed, in the passage quoted a few paragraphs back, that the majority of the people would disapprove of the Society's activities. There were few who even knew about it until he publicized it and his own disapproval of it. Moreover, if the majority had been known in fact to disapprove, Everett was still in the unpleasant position of bowing to tyranny--the tyranny of the majority.

The A.C. L.U. readily understood that the failure of other faculty members to support Teacher Jasper was due to their defenseless position. This was Jasper's first year in that college, yet he had been elected president of the Faculty Forum. The A.C. L.U. noted that 'no evidence existed of Teacher Jasper's inability to get along with his colleagues and superiors prior to the Parnassus controversy.'

It observed however that 'In attempting to evaluate the faculty's attitude after the Parnassus controversy began, it is important to note the lack of a tenure system at (the College). A large part of the faculty is on one-year contract and the rest on three-year contract. Under these circumstances, it is difficult to see how members of the faculty could come to Teacher Jasper's assistance or even remain neutral (emphasis added) without endangering their positions.'

The phrase I have emphasized above made me start with surprise when I first read it. It made me think instantly of the judge in Teacher Quentin's case who made the observation that teachers had 'no rights whatsoever.' I noted that the Civil Liberties Union went much further: teachers not only have no rights; they cannot even remain neutral. They must even betray one of their own number, who may be a friend, when the administration gives the sign. Where, in what human breast, may integrity find a lodging?

I have found only a few teachers who fully understand this helplessness to resist betraying a fellow worker, and almost no persons outside the schools who have even thought about the matter. I wonder if it is possible I have not talked with the right ones--here are at least two persons who understand, the Judge, and the writer of the Civil Liberties Union report. I wonder what even they think while their children are pursuing education in this atmosphere of oppression.

What opportunity have the young ever to develop inquiring minds, integrity, and independence of spirit? They will not develop these qualities of character by being ordered to develop them. They must see these qualities in action in the lives of the adults around them to whom they look for guidance and precedent in their conduct. God help them.

The Civil Liberties Union noted that one of the deans, Administrator Lund, stated that the college employes gave high priority to their own security. It quoted him as saying in a talk to a group of citizens, 'To put it very bluntly and honestly the faculty is concerned about salaries, and they feel that the matter of the college doing a good job in this district is a matter of concern to the people who support it.'

Further, the A.C.L.U. said, 'the lack of a tenure system and the prevalence of one-year contracts makes for an atmosphere of fear and insecurity, and a dependence upon the whims of administrators and the Board.' Whether they realized it or not, the A.C.L.U. here stated the working conditions of employes in every school district in the United States and at least many if not all higher institutions.

Members of the Board, the A.C.L.U. noted, supported the President, and 'showed no awareness of their obligation to interpret the principles of academic freedom to the community.' These views and those of the President, the A.C.L.U. report states, result in these persons 'becoming arbiters of literary value. Moreover, their standard--that literary works may properly be judged by the presence or absence of objectionable words--has long been rejected both by the courts and by competent literary critics.'

These words of the A.C.L.U. stand in sharp relief against the attitude of self-appointed censors of literature in the schools. Taboos change with time but the impulse to censor, to regulate what students and teachers, and everybody else for that matter, may read and discuss remains a constant. I was a high school teacher when I read Rabelais and James Joyce's ULYSSES. I was carefully discreet as to the persons with whom I discussed these books.

When I was a high school journalism teacher in the 1930's I agreed to write reviews of the successive novels of Vardis Fisher's VRIDAR HUNTER TETRALOGY for a local newspaper, but I carefully stipulated that my name was not to be signed to any of them. The newspaper men who accepted this agreement were as intelligent and discerning as those who commented 30 years later on the censorship of the management of Teacher Jasper's college. Yet they could not have saved me in the face of either a public outcry or the censoring instincts of the management of my school. They understood the necessity of my not having a by-line on the reviews. I am now at peace, since it is 30 years too late for those former employers to bring reprisals against me.

Newspaper commentary cited by the A.C.L.U. was critical of administrative tactics bearing on individual rights. One editorial statement was that when a college administration 'concerns itself with the conduct of a staff member in his own home it is stretching authority.'

The home town newspaper of Teacher Jasper's college pointed out that this controversy 'involved the rights of faculty members to have the same freedom to speak and act as any other citizens.' It urged the college to study the matter and mentioned that other higher institutions of learning have developed standard policies on it. Such a study, the editorial writer suggested,

'might determine that people of professional competence in education and in the field being taught would be the best judges of teacher competence;

'might indicate that differences of opinion should not be sufficient cause for discipline;

'might show that a teacher, in his own personal life, has a right to conduct himself in any manner he sees fit, so long as it is legal;

'might indicate it is not the function of a college board, or administrator, to judge all the personal behavior of each faculty member.'

'Such rights,' the editorial continued, 'are not 'far out.' State and federal laws grant them to employes of private industry. . . . Public employes have not enjoyed such rights. If they had them, there might be fewer problems in public administration.'

These editorial comments and similarly critical comments of other newspapers in that sparsely populated college district suggest that people in metropolitan areas may after all not be far in advance in their judgment of bad taste and obscenity.

This scuttling of an energetic college teacher illustrates the dominance of administration in the schools. He and the literary society were suppressed, the President said, to prevent public pressure on the administration. This was the same complaint that deprived Teacher Quentin of his job. Teacher Isaacs was fired for alleged slighting of administrative rules. The pattern of all this opens to question the extent to which schools are institutions of administration rather than institutions of learning.

To develop our subject properly we must at this point look at some of the background of the decline of public attention to teaching and learning, as interest has shifted to administration.

This dominance of administration emerged comparatively recently, in the history of the public schools. It followed the pattern of business organization and consolidation into larger units by merging, which started before World War I and which has accelerated conspicuously since World War II. Schools and colleges of education had a strong influence in this development in the schools as part of their role in the growth of philosophies and theories in educational matters.

An older theory, mentioned in Chapter 5, that administrators and teachers are colleagues, has been overshadowed by the newer one, with its view of a school district as a corporation engaged in education as a business enterprise, with a line-and-staff organization. This was the view of the Engelhardt brothers, two theorists on the subject whose monumental and pioneering studies of school administration 40 years ago have had a permanent effect on the schools.

'A public school system,' they wrote, 'is a business enterprise operating under what might be called a state charter (school laws).'*

Development of school adminstration as a line-and-staff type of organization, taken from business and the military, with its pyramid concept of a school staff hierarchy, is deplored by some school men according to another writer, Harlan L. Hagman.

'Contrary to the desires of many school superintendents,' he said, 'the superintendent and other school administrators were held to be employers and the teachers employes in a management-labor dichotomy which denied the status of the administrator as a teacher among teachers. Communication in the larger systems became one-way and interaction between teachers and administrators became exceedingly difficult even when the administrator actively sought the opinions and participation of teachers in making administrative decisions. The organization seemed to place teaching at the service of administration although the feeling was growing that administration properly viewed was a facilitating service to the teacher-learning situation.'**

Hagman advised school administrators on procedures of separation--i. e., firing--of teachers; he urges that this not be done summarily and that a teacher considered unsatisfactory be warned and given a chance to improve; but he gives no hint of questioning management's prerogative to fire.***

Administrative dominance is illustrated again in a dilemma over democracy. Management must perforce proclaim its devotion to the principles of individual freedom on which this nation is founded. Since the schools have a responsibility to perpetuate this principle by teaching and defending it vigorously, failure to practice it would be a flagrant transgression. Hagman mentioned superintendents who sought teacher participation in making administrative decisions. He may not have realized some of the difficulties. If 50 or 5,000 teachers were to help make a decision they would have to be fully informed of the facts and contingencies and reach a majority consensus after debate and the clash of dissenting opinions.

That teachers are just about the last persons of all to dissent openly in the presence of their employers is well-known.

*Engelhardt, J. L. and Fred Engelhardt. PUBLIC SCHOOL BUSINESS ADMINISTRATION. N. Y.: Teachers College, Columbia University. 1927. p. 8.
**THE ADMINISTRATION OF AMERICAN PUBLIC SCHOOLS. N. Y.: McGraw Hill. 1951. Pp. 33-36.
***Ibid. pp. 220-221.

The prevalence of fear among them is traditional and the reasons for this are certainly not unknown. Readers have observed the causes in the account I have given of Teachers Isaacs, George, and Quentin. In the controversy over Professor Jasper, the reasons are given explicitly by the American Civil Liberties Union. His colleagues did not dare to support him or even remain neutral after he was attacked. Open dissent makes a teacher a marked person whose prospects for a future in school work are not bright.

Most of the textbooks on school administration are directed to the public schools, such as the samples quoted in this chapter; but these samples apply to administration in higher education. The reader has seen in the story of Teacher Jasper how similar the insecurity is, throughout all levels. It will be seen again in the story of Teacher Darrell.

Administrators frequently proclaim that their faculty meetings are democratic, and the teacher associations proclaim on every possible occasion their practice of democracy in all of their affairs. For an example of school management philosophy regarding democratic practices, I cite a passage in Ward G. Reeder's textbook on school administration published in the 1930 edition and the 1958 revised edition:

'Just as there are two types of government, or labor-capital relationship, and of other ways of life in the world today, so there are two types of school administration. These are: first, the autocratic type; second, the democratic type.'*

In the autocratic type 'the superintendent hands down orders, consults nobody, expects unquestioning obedience, talks of my department, my school, my principals.'*

In democratic administration the superintendent 'desires to be known as a brother of his employes rather than a 'boss.'

'Each school administrator must decide for himself which type of administration he will practice.'*

Here is the explicit statement that the superintendent has the power to be democratic or autocratic at will with his faculty. He can at will turn democracy on and off. This by definition is a contradiction, indeed in a very elementary way. Some teachers at least will know full well he may turn 'democracy' on at the beginning of a discussion and turn it off at any time after or even during the meeting.

*THE FUNDAMENTALS OF PUBLIC SCHOOL ADMINISTRATION. N. Y. : Macmillan. Quoted passages are on pp. 8-9 in 1930 ed. Reeder's emphasis.

A historian recognized this fallacy in the effort of Great Britain during the first decade of this century to introduce some self-government in India without giving up full power of final decision.

'The desire of the British government to introduce an element of representative government,' he wrote, 'while, at the same time, maintaining complete control over all policy made the reforms a contradiction within themselves.' *

It is disconcerting to me that an accepted authority, the author of a textbook in his professional field, perpetrates such an obvious fallacy as this, and even more so that leaders in the educational hierarchy accept the authority and base their practice on such an untenable proposition. That such persons are as confused as this on a fundamental principle of our way of life is disturbing. It is hardly to be expected that business executives, competent as they may well be in their own field, are the best qualified persons to govern the nation's intellectual and cultural pursuits.

President Everett seemed to subordinate this government to the will of the majority, which can all too often mean the whim or caprice of the majority. Educational and cultural leadership, it seems to me, however it may at times have to bow to the will of the majority, should yet not be ready to surrender to it, but should have the will and capacity to influence it to higher and more liberalized levels, and also to resist the tyranny of the majority. It should insist on the rights of individuals and not merely a tolerance but a profound respect for honest differences of opinion.

This is the point of the Civil Liberties Union's reference to the College Board's 'obligation' to interpret the principles of academic freedom to the community. In this respect for dissent is found the essence of democracy.

A surrender of educational management to ignorance and bigotry carries the faculty down with it; for a faculty which because of its insecurity cannot even remain neutral toward a colleague threatened by intolerance likewise can hardly assume leadership in intellectual and cultural emancipation in the face of the all-powerful management's abdication of responsibility.

*Wallbank, T. Walter. A SHORT HISTORY OF INDIA AND PAKISTAN. N. Y.: New American Library of World Literature. 1958. (paperback). Pp. 114-115.

Chapter 11

HIGHER EDUCATION: ATTRITION

The 'fear and insecurity' among teachers, mentioned by the American Civil Liberties Union, are not all due to the lack of tenure. Even if fear and insecurity are not as great among teachers in higher education as in faculties of the public schools, they are an ever present problem and do great mischief. I have shown in the story of Teacher Kelly that tenure is not a very strong bar against an enterprising school administration's getting rid of a teacher. Neither is it an impregnable bulwark of security for a long-established, brilliantly successful university professor, as I shall show in this next case study.

I allude to Teacher Darrell and begin his story here. Even a painfully condensed account of this teacher's experience demonstrates that management holds the power and exercises it at will. Teacher Darrell had been an outstanding professor in his university for 20 years when the blows began to fall. His classes year after year had attracted large numbers of students, sometimes more than 200, many of them not majoring in his field but drawn to him by his magnetic power to lead them into the exciting adventure of learning. Yet the management of the university, whose President I am calling Administrator Kane Morton, maneuvered to reduce these classes to a mere handful, then gave the courses Teacher Darrell had developed to other faculty members, and finally abolished them.

I have never met Professor Darrell. My information about this case is from reading his published statement, newspaper articles, long acquaintance and frequent conversations with one of his former students, and my correspondence with him.

I do not know why Professor Darrell was singled out for The Treatment. The story discloses clues, which I shall not pursue. The substance is in the plain facts. He was subjected to administrative abuses for a decade, beginning about 1947, and the after effects were still much in evidence well into the 1960's. Some years after the start his name was dropped from the faculty list of his department, Journalism, though not from the general list in the University Catalog. Students who asked to be enrolled in his classes were told that he was no longer teaching them.

These and other circumstances eventually attracted the attention of the public through newspaper stories. Many alumni wrote letters of protest to the university and the newspapers. My wife and I, living 3,000 miles from this university, read stories in the newspapers about the affair. We became interested when a young woman friend of ours who had been one of Professor Darrell's students received a letter from him with an account of some of The Treatment. She started to read this letter in the presence of my wife, then suddenly burst into tears and exclaimed 'They can't do this to him! He taught me to think!'

She explained that his teaching had been the great influence in her life, the inspiring force that had given direction to her purposes, such that she had achieved some long-range goals, including being a newspaper woman earning her living by writing.

At about the time The Treatment began, the administration was launching a project to transform the journalism program to a trade school status, in which the liberal arts and intellectual content of Teacher Darrell's courses would be incongruous. The first stroke of administrative Treatment of which I am aware was pressure from Administrator Gregg Queen, a dean, that Teacher Darrell must go back to school for two more quarters of graduate study. In this demand the dean may have overlooked the fact that a person who has enthusiasm for his intellectual pursuits and has an inquiring mind automatically grows more by these labors than in almost any other way.

Administrator Queen had recommended to President Morton that Teacher Darrell be acting head of the journalism department for the time being, and be actual head with the rank of full professor upon completion of the graduate study. Administrator Morton seemed to approve this recommendation, but with oblique phrasing. He wrote to Queen 'under the conditions you mention, he (Teacher Darrell) may look forward to becoming head of the department with the rank of full professor.' Although he did not say explicitly 'will be head of the department,' his statement was assumed to be a commitment.

A little over a year later Teacher Darrell reported to the President that he had completed a 'substantial portion' of the required graduate study and reminded him that he was to be made department head. After another year, however, in 1949, when Professor Darrell had completed more than the specified amount of graduate study, and when the department had been converted into a division of the College of Arts and Sciences, Administrator Morton instructed the dean of this college, Administrator Ashley Randall, to 'select and recommend for appointment a director of the Journalism Division.'

A day later Teacher Darrell inquired of Morton by letter whether this instruction to Randall 'is meant to contain any element of uncertainty as to the intention of the University to meet fully its commitment to me.' The President answered that he questioned whether Darrell's studies 'have fulfilled completely the letter and spirit of the requirement as I understand it.' He added, 'I have caused your name to be listed as full professor.' Morton took the position that changing journalism from a department to a division nullified the commitment that Darrell would be in charge of it. At this point Darrell made a conciliatory concession; he offered to permit the university to 'modify' this part of the commitment if it kept faith with the rest--making him full professor and allowing him to continue the courses he had developed.

Administrator Morton's reply was that Darrell should settle this matter with the Director of the Journalism Division. 'Of course,' he wrote, 'full recognition of your work in building up the department will be taken into account.'

Darrell said he was primarily interested in continuing the courses he had developed and taught for many years. On Aug. 1, 1949 President Morton wrote to him: 'The University recognizes and appreciates your work in the development of Journalism up to its position of recognized worth. Many of the features of the program spring from the distinctive emphasis in your own teaching. As we agreed in our conference these distinctive developments in your courses will be preserved through your continuing responsibility for teaching them.'

This would seem to have settled the matter. The President went one step further in this letter, in an apparent move to

90

make the situation more cheerful. He wrote, 'It is assumed that the Director will look to you for a great deal of information and counsel.'

In the two years this controversy had continued, letters of inquiry and concern from alumni and others had been arriving in the offices of the persons involved. The following statements in two of Administrator Morton's responses to these inquiries indicate his efforts at reassurance:

Letter dated Aug. 23, 1949: 'You may be sure that there is no desire or intention whatsoever to discredit the work of Teacher Darrell. We recognize the peculiar contributions which he has made in this field and shall expect to see him develop them further.'

Letter of Sept. 22, 1949: 'There is, of course, no idea of destroying or making ineffective the work of Professor Darrell. His distinctive contribution will continue to be made although that will be but one phase of our enlarged program.'

This expansion included a great proliferation of courses and 'sequences'--i. e., major programs--and faculty members in the journalism division, accompanied by a proportionately rapid and steady decline in the quantity and quality of enrollment, until there was difficulty in finding assignments for all the faculty.

Administrator Morton's vagueness is evident in these assurances as it was in his 'may look forward' phrase. Such terms as 'peculiar contributions' and 'shall expect to see him develop it further' are capable of various interpretations.

Letters from alumni to Teacher Darrell expressed indignation at the treatment to which he was being subjected. Some of them also congratulated him on a signal honor he had received, dedication of the 1950 student yearbook to him. Among the letter writers were newspaper men and women, members of publishing and magazine editorial offices, novelists and other free lance writers, and other alumni of professional stature.

Two and a half years after the hectic summer of 1949 the University Committee on Professional Relations and Standards supported Teacher Darrell in a report to the President on findings in an investigation of the controversy. This report, dated Jan. 9, 1952, pointed out that although Professor Darrell had been given full professorial rank, his salary was only $5,700 a year 'as against the present median of $6,500 at (the University), actually less than the highest salaries paid here in the next lower rank.'

Correction of this inequity was urged, 'not only for itself but also because it focuses attention on salary equity problems in general, involving recognition and rank, seniority, and quality of service without undue discrimination between established professors and new additions or between men and women in comparable posts.' Nine committee members signed the report. The committee also declared that if Teacher Darrell's problem should be presented to the University Board of Control, the report should be one of the exhibits.

This involvement of a faculty committee is a reminder of Parkinson's Law in the operation of which officials of an organization make work for each other; the bigger the organization, the more officials there are to make more work for each other. In this case it begins when someone starts to meddle with Professor Darrell, who has simply been doing his job. Then this meddling involves another person, then still another. The professor's performance suffers and this involves still other persons--the Faculty Committee, the University Board of Control, and interested and outraged alumni and other citizens, including the person writing this book 3,000 miles away.

As the Professor's effectiveness is diminished, the volume of time and energy expended rises in geometric progression where no energy at all was required before. This continues for years. When the whole storm finally blows over everybody goes back to his own affairs and the Professor picks up the pieces and starts teaching again at the point where he had been forced to stop some years before.

This is a prodigious waste of energy and talents and money, all of which needs to be expended for the benefit of the young.

At some time during these exchanges of letters and memoranda among Darrell and the various university officials, Administrator Morton completed the nullification of his commitment to make Darrell head of Journalism, appointing Administrator Keith Olmstead to the post with the title of director. This development and, a little later, nullification of the entire commitment to Darrell brought this decade-long episode to its climax in the summer of 1953, that is, in the classic manner, at about the mid-point of the whole action.

A spate of 'memos' involving Teacher Darrell and Admin-

92

istrators Morton and Olmstead that summer recorded:

A. The simultaneous expansion of the journalism faculty and course offerings, and a sharply declining success in attracting students.

B. A breakdown of orderly procedures and policy in the journalism division, including arbitrary course offerings and assignments.

C. Abolition of Teacher Darrell's courses, completing the repudiation of the commitment.

D. Irregularities in the catalog listing of courses.

E. Adventitious appearance of a 'Bureau of Media Research and Services.'

F. Withdrawal of all class assignments to Darrell.

G. Omission of Darrell's name from the Journalism faculty list in the university catalog.

One curious episode almost like comic opera was a series of notes from Administrator Olmstead to Teacher Darrell demanding that Darrell answer whether or not he accepted his assignments. Darrell answered each one, saying he did accept them and had never intimated anything to the contrary. These repeated demands and reassuring affirmative replies almost seem lifted from musical comedy; suggesting a bass-baritone, rising to fortissimo, demanding 'Do you accept the assignments? Do you, do you, do you?' And the ringing tenor answers, 'Yes, I do accept them, I do, I do, I do.'

Darrell's final note to Olmstead might be conceived as a recitative in reproachful largo, ending the scene: 'I am sorry I have not found it possible to deal with these complex professional matters in the peremptory manner you suggest and I hope you will be indulgent in my effort to be accurate and clear rather then perfunctory and sweeping.'

Chapter 12

HIGHER EDUCATION: DEMOLITION AND SALVAGE

Administrator Morton completed the nullification by shift-
ing the responsibility elsewhere. Keeping the agreement, he
said to Darrell, would 'freeze' the curriculum; and teaching
schedules are made by the dean. In a response dated Sept.
16, 1953 Darrell agreed this was the correct procedure according to the University constitution. Then he raised the
point that the dean, Administrator Olmstead, had repeatedly
violated the constitution by unilateral actions bypassing the
faculty and not leaving records of actions taken.

About a month later he reminded the President that no
classes were currently assigned to him, and reminded that
a year earlier he had predicted this was likely to happen. A
few weeks later Professor Darrell pointed out to the University Board of Control that during this same school year, while
course offerings, sequences, faculty members, and the budget
for Journalism had been increased enormously, enrollment in
Basic Reporting, required of all beginning journalism major
students, had plummeted from 62 students in 1948-1949 to a
mere 12 in 1952-1953.

At this point Darrell filed an appeal of the case to the University Board, citing violations of the University Constitution
by the Journalism dean in dropping and adding courses,
changing faculty assignments, and allowing graduation of students whose scholastic records were below grade level requirements. He pointed out duplication of courses already
offered in other departments, and continuance of courses
for which there was almost no demand. He informed the
Board of the arbitrary creation of the Bureau of Media Research and Service 'without reference to or authorization of
the faculty of the school.'

Comparing the Journalism program with that of this university's sister school in the same State, he cited the Board

of Control's own records for Spring 1953, showing total journalism enrollment in his school was 29 as compared with 64 in the sister school; the number of courses was 60, to 33 in the other school; and sequences 12, to four in the sister school. In the face of vanishing student interest the cost of journalism had increased 'many hundred per cent.'

In 1954 Darrell was given no assignments, his name was omitted from the journalism faculty list, and the dean refused to allow students to enroll with him for individual instruction. Darrell spent his time in research for the Bureau of Media Research and Services of questioned legitimacy. In this he was hampered by administrative neglect to provide promised materials and clerical help.

The Board of Control responded by reappointing him professor of journalism, but he was not notified of the fact; he learned it only after two letters of inquiry to the university president. The latter, in the meantime, gave Darrell repeated statements that he was trying to find a means of giving him teaching assignments 'that will appear to be satisfactory.' It seems curious to me that he did not say simply 'that will be satisfactory.'

These labors brought Darrell an assignment in the Spring of 1955 to teach freshman English in a nearby military base. There was talk of sending him to a similar job on another military base 900 miles away on an island in the Ocean. I do not know what effect these years of prolonged harassment had on Professor Darrell's morale. His experience must have revealed to him that teachers are but helpless pieces of the game some administrators play. A more effective technique of harassing would have been the reverse of depriving him of teaching duties; it would have been to give him such a heavy teaching load that he would have had little time to carry on his defense.

However, his teaching services continued to go to waste during 1954, 1955, and 1956. Finally on Dec. 13, 1956 came the crisis in this real-life 10-year drama. On that date Administrator Morton addressed a letter to Teacher Darrell reporting that efforts to transfer him to another department had failed and that Administrator Olmstead was 'not willing to reassign you to the courses you taught formerly, nor to any other courses in the curriculum.'

He said that Olmstead 'concludes his report with the recommendation that your membership on the staff of the School

of Journalism be terminated at the close of the current year...
ending June 30, 1957, in which recommendation I concur.'

Teacher Darrell twice asked the President, on Dec. 17, 1956
and Jan. 7, 1957, for a written statement of particulars of the
charges against him. The President answered the second of
these queries in a letter dated Jan. 9, 1957, saying, 'I conclude
that the case is one of failure to cooperate with the Dean and
exhibiting an attitude of antagonism to the program of the Dean
of the School of Journalism of the University.'

Darrell's reply five days later opened with: 'Your letter of
Jan. 9, addressed to my home but unstamped, reached me
through campus mail today.' The failure to stamp the letter
could have been, of course, an accident. He said of the accusations, 'Your attention is called to Article VIII, Section A,
3, a, of the University Constitution which stipulates that an
action for dismissal must be based on specific charges and
such specific charges furnished the faculty member accused.
Obviously a loose and unspecified charge of 'failure to cooperate' could be applied to almost anyone who ever happened to differ with the accuser; equally obviously, the charge,
when unspecified, may well be a virtue; a free society or a
free university is incompatible with an army of 'yes-men.'
The all-important thing in 'cooperation' is the specific instance.'

Professor Darrell was notably gentle in this missive. He
might have written: I expect from you a written statement of
the particulars of my alleged act or acts of non-cooperation
and antagonism, specifying the date of each.

The two administrators here appear as blood brothers of
public school administrators. Their actions seem to stem
from the same assumption of administrative prerogative,
dispensing with such nonsense as evidence. One wonders if
their graduate degrees might be Doctor of Education.

It seems to me disconcerting that a university president
would need to be told elementary principles of adjudicating a
dispute. The accused professor scored another palpable hit
in this letter. Since he was not teaching, the administration
had asked him to engage in research for the unauthorized but
administratively convenient Bureau of Media Research and
Services and suggested he propose a subject. Darrell proposed 'as being timely as well as having general and lasting
value, a study of the views of editors, journalists, writers,
publicists, and students of the press, on the subject of the
proper education of journalists.'

In view of the disastrous collapse of the journalism school that had been taken out of his hands after his service in building it, this subject assuredly was timely; and it could hardly have been rejected or hailed with pleasure by the university administration. Our main concern here, however, must be with the accusations against Darrell and his comments on them.

What constitutes a fair and honest and competent accusation? Most citizens have at least some notion of established judicial practice: an accused person has a right to know not only the accusations but the grounds on which they are based; to know who the accusers are and to face them in open public proceedings; and to have competent counsel, and reasonable time to prepare his defense.

All this is fundamental in court procedures. The crucial point here is whether these rights are inherent for persons other than those brought into a court of justice. Do the courts grant these rights merely for convenience as a modus operandi? Certainly not: they recognize them as inherent rights of any accused person in any circumstances. It ought to be totally unnecessary to raise this issue before American readers, the traditions of our nation being what they are; but disregard of the issue in high places forces attention to it. These rights are inherent in the pursuit of justice for all persons on all occasions, whom accusation places in jeopardy, whether in a court of law or anywhere else.

The long established practice in schools of accepting mere statement of an administrator against a teacher as sufficient to disqualify the teacher supported Administrator Morton. How deeply this practice is embedded is illustrated in an incident that happened in California in 1961. This State had just enacted the law to protect probationary teachers which the Judge found ineffective for Teacher Quentin. An association of school administrators had gathered to hear an attorney explain this law.

One of the administrators asked, 'Do you need evidence?' This ineffective law will yet accomplish some good if it influences school people in particular and citizens generally to think about evidence, its meaning and uses, and about inherent rights of accused persons.

Final note on Teacher Darrell: it is pleasant to report that he survived the decade of continued, mounting assaults which threatened to scuttle his career. It would be pleasanter if one could also report that his survival was due to an orderly procedure of adjudication in which the merits of the case were determined by the evidence. It would be pleasanter still if one could say that there was full redress for all the indignities heaped upon him and for the loss suffered by students who for years were deprived of his services.

All this would be too much to hope for. I should think his calm reasonableness in matchless defense saved him from being done in. But he might yet have been cashiered if the case had not been closed by adventitious circumstances. President Morton retired. One of his last acts of office, in the very last meeting with the Board of Control on the eve of his retirement, was to submit Administrator Olmstead's recommendation with his concurrence, that Darrell's tenure in Journalism be ended. The Board voted to retain Darrell on the University faculty. Soon after, the Board performed a sweeping demolition. It abolished the School of Journalism. Teacher Darrell joined another department, where he resumed teaching the courses he had developed and taught with brilliance for so many years.

So much, then was salvaged. There could never be redress for the loss of years. Some other wrongs remain unrighted: the loss of the Journalism Department under his direction; the fact that into the mid-1960's his salary had never been brought up to the level of his rank and years of service. Nevertheless his victory against overwhelming odds is noteworthy. Such victories, even though they are only of individuals, bring about some restraint; especially they give other brave souls encouragement to resist encroachment of all-too-often insensitive administration into delicate matters where their heavy hand will be only destructive.

It must still be borne in mind that such individual successes leave the power structure intact. Relief must come through modification of this structure. How this should be done is a matter beyond the scope of this book. All citizens are responsible for education and the expenditure of their money to pay for it. They will have to think seriously about the problem and contribute to its solution.

Chapter 13

THE ETHICS PROBLEM

One of my illuminating experiences of undergraduate college days was an introductory course in Ethics. This is a field related in many persons' minds to philosophy. Some regard ethics as a science.

I was fascinated by both the content of this field of learning, that is the principles and ideas of right and just individual conduct, and by the sources of this material from men of many races and cultures in all ages of recorded history. It was an important step in my enlightenment to learn that the Judaeo-Christian tradition is not the only source, and that indeed the principles of decent human conduct are not the property of any one culture or cult, religious or otherwise; they are true and valid in their own right.

I do not know when the schoolmen became interested in establishing a code of professional ethics for themselves. During my intermittent years of teaching up to 1947, and many summers of graduate study, I heard nothing that I can recall about professional ethics for teachers. My duty, as I understood it, was simply to strive to be a good teacher and a decent human being.

When I was assigned full-time as a newsman to the education beat in 1954, the picture had changed. Schoolmen seemed to be having a field day with professional ethics. I heard about it often, especially when there was a personnel problem. It seemed there were rules on every hand: this you must do, that you must not do.

Persons who have read this book thus far may have observed that I was sometimes perplexed in trying to reconcile this professional ethics with what I had learned about ethics in college and in my subsequent reading, thought, and experience with the problems of right conduct towards one's fellow human beings.

The National Education Association and its multitudes of divisions and affiliates have developed a code of professional ethics with the avowed aim of defining and establishing rules and standards of conduct of members such as would be deemed worthy of persons of professional status. Inevitably this code becomes deeply involved in the job status and the personnel problems of teachers.

The particular aspect of this Professional Ethics with which this book is mainly concerned is that which applies to relations between employers and employes, particularly administrators and classroom teachers. It is well known that some other occupational groups, particularly the professions such as law and medicine, have their own ethical codes.

Considered on the level of philosophy these codes are intended, I presume, to apply the principles of general ethical conduct to the particular problems and exigencies of members of the profession. These codes could not, of course, be considered (still in philosophy and theory) as something aside from, or above, or different from the standard established principles of ethics. Such a code cannot be a set of principles which are new or different from the general principles of right conduct which have been discovered out of human experience through the ages, and which even in antiquity were stated by men of the deepest wisdom and widest and most profound knowledge and greatest sensitivity to the problems and dilemmas of mankind.

Rather, the code for persons of a particular occupation must be an adaptation of the general principles of ethics to their peculiar circumstances. Ethical codes for professionals, then, should impose on them, if this is possible, a more stringent, more severe requirement of righteous conduct, than that of the commonalty of men, or at least a more lively striving to achieve such conduct.

With this in mind, we have now to deal with the manner in which school management, in my observation, has used the educational code of ethics in disputes with teachers. Some of this has been shown in the case studies already reported. For instance in the breaking of Teacher Kelly's tenure two high officials of a state teacher association refused to take into account the activities of several administrators which this teacher and her supporters, and I as well, could not construe as civil behavior in any sense.

If this behavior was actually decent, the failure of the officials to try to enlighten the teacher was a breach of ethical obligation. If the behavior was not civil, the failure to condemn it was patently wrong. If the issue was in doubt, the case should have been investigated, or at least the doubt should have been justified. If the failure of the high ethics officials to act at all, even to clarify their position, was in accord with their code of professional ethics, then this professional ethics can hardly be true ethics at all, but something else being passed off as ethics. Under the circumstances the question arises whether the code is an instrument of administrative domination.

Other instances are easily at hand. Teacher Orville Goodwin, for example, was ordered by his superintendent to vacate the school premises and establish himself in an abandoned chicken house on an otherwise vacant plot of ground privately owned. I doubt that the association could have been unaware of this bizarre episode and its unflattering reflection on the teaching profession. Teacher Goodwin procured the consent of the owner before setting up his 'office' in the chicken house. Teachers Howard Lake and Alden Henry abandoned teaching after being fired for vague, trivial reasons, and undertook to support themselves and their families by selling real estate.

Lake remarked to me that he loved teaching and looked upon it as an art. He said he wanted to practice his art as artists traditionally do, regardless of the monetary reward. My many years of teaching and association with other teachers had prepared me to hear this statement without the least surprise. In 20 years of teaching in high school and junior college, between September, 1920 and June, 1946, my income was always less than $1,800 a year.

Though this was scrimpy, and though I have been happy to see teachers' salaries rise to a more decent level in recent years, I must still maintain that the low income was never a major cause of teachers leaving the schools. I am convinced there have always been plenty of capable persons who would have been content to remain in the schools permanently at the prevailing salaries if their jobs had been stable and their working conditions reasonable. The increasing pressure for higher salaries in recent years--with which I am wholly in sympathy--has been due mainly to the failure to look into working conditions. Teaching, working with the young in their pursuit of learning, is a delightful, richly rewarding occupation when the conditions of work are favorable.

One administrative criticism of Henry was that he was 'too

101

enthusiastic.' Teacher Everett Charles resigned after harrowing treatment by management. His superintendent demanded that he withdraw his resignation so that the school board could have the satisfaction of firing him. His appeals to the association were ignored. Years afterward he wrote that it still upset him to be reminded of this experience.

In contemplating these and numerous similar incidents I find the thought recurring that the code of ethics seems intended for teachers, and largely exempts administrators. Even if the code endorses the administrative prerogative of of absolute control of jobs--and of course it does in practice-- I do not understand how it can ignore the tactics.

A decade after Teacher Kelly began experiencing the tenuousness of her tenure as related earlier in this book she was again subjected to The Treatment--in another school district, of course--during the course of which professional ethics was one of the instruments of harassment.

A year or two prior to this, Teacher Harry Elliott found himself involved in a dispute with his administration and the association, during which he was accused of violating ethics in some of his acts. He replied that his ideas of ethics were different from those of his accusers.

Teacher Kelly's difficulties began in what might be termed a classic situation, a change of administration. This change occurred in 1962. After being forced out of her tenure job in 1955 she had accepted a teaching position in another school district with the full realization, she acknowledged, that teaching is not a career, as she had previously regarded it, but a year-to-year chance occupation.

She was pleased to find in her new job an administration that truly wanted good teaching and understood it is to be had only when teachers have freedom as individuals, without which initiative and enthusiasam for creative work cannot flourish. She enjoyed the ebullient, friendly atmosphere engendered by the freedom. She was admired by her fellow teachers and especially appreciated by the inexperienced ones, who found her a willing source of ready help with their problems. She made a wide circle of friends among the community's citizens.

In the Spring of 1962 she was completing her fourth year in that district. (There had been and interlude of three years in another.) Her assignments had not been easy. Being known as a master teacher, she was given classes heavily loaded

102

with difficult youngsters. She sometimes remarked ruefully that she seemed to be regarded as a specialist with troubled pupils. In accordance with her long-established practice she never refused any pupil assigned to her and never asked to have a pupil removed from her class. She enjoyed a wide diversity of nationalities among the youngsters of the school.

She well knew, when the change of administration came in 1962, that such a shift usually brings about drastic changes, of spirit, philosophy, and personnel. Nevertheless, come September, she returned to the pleasant environs of the school, located in the lower levels of a mountain range on the eastern outskirts of a city. The morning view of the valley and the mountains beyond to the west was always charming; it was stimulating, in looking down on the pall of smog which hid the city, to know one was in the cleaner air above it.

The afternoon view was equally pleasing, with the swinging, curving mountain ridges to the east cast in bold relief by shadows and slanting sunlight. Perhaps this September day marked the beginning of one more year of comparative tranquility, before the new administration began in earnest the inevitable work of breaking up the old established, peaceful, and harmonious relationships it had inherited from its predecessor. She had little doubt that this breakup would come; for when a superintendent resigns under pressure he is usually a scapegoat for community disharmony whether or not he was in any way responsible for it.

And so, what about the scapegoat's successor? You must see that he is in an advantageous position; the people are excited and upset; hence drastic changes do not disturb them as much as in quiet times. Yet he must not move too suddenly. He needs time, perhaps a year or so, to become acquainted with the district and to find out the moves he can make with greatest safety. Teachers are uneasy and restive; some will resign merely because the former superintendent, whom they trusted and who supported them, is gone; some others can be encouraged to resign by a little subtle maneuvering here and there. It might be well to make a small beginning by getting rid of a few minor administrators such as principals, especially any who were close to the preceding superintendent.

Somewhat to her surprise, Teacher Kelly started the year with a class made up almost entirely of well-adjusted youngsters eager to learn. This was the first class of this character that had been assigned to her for several years and it was pleasant. During the first semester she remarked several times rather whimsically that this agreeable assignment could not last.

It didn't. In the middle of the year she was one day told abruptly that she would have to move the next week to another of the district's three schools and take charge of a new group of pupils in a different grade from that of her present class. Her new pupils had been selected from three large classes. She found many of them difficult to manage. This was the sign; the pattern was about to be repeated. She had been singled out for The Treatment. There was no choice unless she chose to resign.

She decided she could endure the situation until the end of the year. With her background of experience, her concern was not the difficult pupils but difficult management. There was a particular point in staying because she would have tenure if she were rehired. It would be interesting to see what the management would do about that. Her teaching days were numbered in that district and almost certainly in any district; this she had learned in her previous protracted experience with The Treatment eight years before. She knew she was only a year-to-year teacher until the joys of this absorbing occupation should end under the blows of wretched personnel practices.

She determined to be of tough enough fiber to endure the ordeal again to study more closely the techniques of harassment. She took charge of the new class of difficult pupils, and taught it with complete success for the remainder of the year.

The new administration dropped its mask on May 13, 1963. This was a crucial date, for under school law a teacher was automatically rehired unless notified to the contrary not later than May 15. Teacher Kelly had thought the signs indicated she would be notified of dismissal; but that date came and went, and after the Ides of May she was automatically rehired and on tenure. Management has the means, however, of dampening one's gratification on achieving this goal. Management handed Teacher Kelly a bountiful shower of left-handed compliments.

It wrote her a letter on that May 13 date expressing ostensible misgivings about rehiring her, and ordering her to an executive meeting of the Board of Trustees. The board apparently intended to put the letter in Teacher Kelly's hands on the May 13 date but failed to do so. She received it when she

attended the board executive session on May 20, too late to
deny her tenure if that was its intent.

Readers may examine this letter of uncomplimentary questions, including its shortcomings of grammar and rhetoric
but excluding indentifying names. It is the subject of the next
chapter.

Chapter 14

ETHICS: THE BASHFUL SCHOOL BOARD

This is the letter, with identifying words excluded:

May 13, 1963

Teacher Kelly
(Street Address)
(City, State)

Dear Teacher Kelly:

The Board of Trustees of _____ School District
wishes to make known to you some of the areas of concern
regarding your employment as a permanent teacher for the
1963-'64 school year.

1. Grading Philosophy

Is your grading policy consistent with the established
philosophy of the _____ School District? Does the
report card grade given by you objectively reflect the
pupils (sic) academic achievement based on a grade level
standard? Can you justify pupils (sic) achievement
grades to principal and parent in terms of daily work,
periodic tests, and assigned grade level expectancy?

2. Teaching Procedures and Practices

Is instruction done in small group situations whenever
possible? Are short and long range lesson plans, in all
areas, available for substitute teachers and for inspection by the school and district administrators upon request? Are all pupils given the daily specified minutes
of instruction in all academic areas? Is your teaching
day divided into periods for each required subject? Are
children required to participate in all subjects regard-

106

less of their personal mood at the time it is (sic) scheduled? Are pupils expected to perform operationally in
your classroom in such a manner that (sic) allows them
to adjust easily to the routine and procedures of most
teachers they might meet the following year?

3. Professional Responsibilities

Are you consistently ethical and professional in your
comments regarding school and district personnel? Do
you attend all (emphasis in original) meetings called by
district administrators where attendance is either ordered or implied? Do you accept the fact that all teachers are employed by the governing board and may be
assigned to teach in any school or grade within the district?

An affirmative answer to the above questions and in
practice (emphasis in original) of the underlying philosophy, just as all other rules and regulations of the district, becomes a part of the signed teaching contract and
conformity with this philosophy will be expected of all
teachers returning to the district for the 1963-'64 school
year.

Very truly yours,

----------School District Governing Board

_____
_____
_____
_____
_____

This is to certify that a conference was held
with the governing board at which time the
contents of this letter were made known to me.

_____
Teacher Kelly

The five blank spaces above were for signature of the five
board members. There are three signatures on the original

of this letter.

No administrator or board member had discussed with Teacher Kelly her performance during the year. None had complained to her of any shortcomings in her work. This letter was thrust into her hands without forewarning. The school district management raised the issues in these twelve questions on the eve of granting her tenure and persisted with them after granting tenure. These questions had been in somebody's mind for some time but had not been communicated to the teacher. Yet the board demanded that she answer them at once in that executive session.

This tentative, hesitant letter stands in sharp contrast to the decisive prosecution of The Treatment which deprived Teacher Kelly of her tenure job in 1956. Whoever wrote these furtive, bumbling questions, beating about like a tongue-tied, bashful boy, the trustees accepted responsibility for it. The board could have asked the administration the questions about Teacher Kelly. They concern matters for which the administration is paid to be informed.

As to the question of being 'consistently ethical and professional,' these matters would be regarded by the educational hierarchy as its domain rather than that of the lay trustees. The letter says nothing about what basis there may have been for this or any other of the questions. These questions--all twelve of them--originated from somebody's covert purpose. If the management had been candid, its first step would have been to state point by point the grounds of its doubts about this teacher. These school management men questioned Teacher Kelly's ethics; readers may have some opinion of theirs.

Well, where else than in the schools would an employer write a letter like this to an employe he intended or hoped to dismiss? It is simply inconceivable in any other field of work. I look back on my years in various kinds of employment and in all of them such a letter would have been the wildest incongruity. I was fired a few times and I have witnessed the firing of other men.

These dismissals were brief, very brief and direct. Often there was anger; I have heard exchanges of hot words. But pomp and ceremony, a string of twelve questions on a variety of insinuations but affirming nothing--I have never heard of such a thing.

If the school trustees had done as other employers typically do to get an unpleasant job off their backs without a mess to clean up afterwards they might have spoken to the teacher or had their superintendent speak, not write, somewhat as follows, (if they felt they had to say as much as there is in this letter):

'Teacher Kelly, we are thinking of firing you. We think you don't grade the way we want grading done. We don't believe you grade according to what the pupils have learned, or that you can prove you have done this.

'You haven't taught the pupils in small groups, as we want done. We don't believe you have written lesson plans for the school officers to read or that you teach all pupils all subjects. You don't have periods in the day for all subjects and make the pupils pay attention accordingly regardless of how they feel, or get them ready to behave with the teacher they will have next year.

'You gossip about other people in the school behind their backs. You don't attend staff meetings and you seem to think you don't have to take whatever assignments we give you.

'You've got to realize that the contract says we tell you what to do and you have got to obey.'

Most of the dismissals I have observed were accomplished in fewer than one tenth as many words as the above; I tried to cover as many points as there are in the letter; perhaps not the identical points, as I am not sure I understand all of the vagueness in the letter.

I have wondered whether the five board members, especially the three who signed the letter, thought of comparing this way of dealing with unwanted employes with the way employers in other kinds of work deal with them. Some of the board members must surely have had experience in employment fields other than the schools. How could they not see the incongruity?

There is nothing about the letter--contents, manner, or phraseology--to indicate that it originated with the board members. It reeks of educational pussyfooting and jargon. If all five board members had grievances against the teacher, as this letter represents, they could have handled them in the normal civil manner with a straightforward confrontation explaining fully the grounds of their discontent, answering all questions the defendant might have until there could be no

109

doubt on any point, and allowing her decent time to take counsel and prepare to defend herself.

This proper procedure in a grievance puts the supposed offender in a position to exonerate himself if the accusers are in error, or make amends if he is at fault, or prepare his defenses if there is disagreement. He must have reasonable time to give these matters careful thought and planning and to take counsel. After this, if there is still disagreement the issue is fairly joined and both parties are free to proceed on the basis of mutually known facts. The accuser has the choice of dropping the matter or prosecuting it further for redress. This principle lies at the base of our system of jurisprudence.

More than that, it is a basic principle of decent human relations, i. e., ethics.

This letter uses an old, old trick to catch the unwary and defenseless--the trick of attempting to incite an adversary into entangling himself by instant refutation and defense. In such a circumstance anything he says or does provides the plotters with material they can turn against him. They can combine against the single individual in testifying what was said and done in such a star chamber session.

There is no custom or precedent or law to protect a teacher against such a cowardly attack as this.

And out of this mess of garbage comes, of all things, an appeal to ethics. This picture of cravens sniping at the defenseless and invoking ethics the while is not adequately characterized by comparison with noisome garbage. My shorter Oxford English Dictionary gives in its definition of 'obscene,' 'Offensive to the senses or the mind.' There let the matter rest. The letter is obscene.

It seems to me inconceivable that an employer in industry would ask one of his employes, such as a salesman, miner, engineer, or electrician, 'Are you consistently ethical and professional in your comments regarding personnel of this company?' O, this just couldn't happen; but supposing it could, I think I'd like to be there, but in a safe place, to witness the explosion.

If education means anything at all of worth, its very core is learning to practice the rules of decent conduct toward fellow human beings, beginning in--and before--kindergarten.

We are not yet finished with this letter. The ideas and

language are those of the schoolman. Anyone familiar with the writing of the educators will recognize this in the phrases and very tone. 'Areas of concern,' 'grade level expectancy,' 'daily specified minutes of instruction,' and 'in practice of this underlying philosophy' literally reek of educational jargon. Perhaps the solecisms require no comment.

I have information of other occasions on which school boards and administrators have resorted to tactics such as these of badgering a lone teacher in executive sessions. If similar games are arranged against employes in other occupations as a standard practice they have not come to my attention. One would expect an employer to find out rather soon whether an employe is responsible and capable. If he is, what more does the employer want? If he does not choose to give an outstanding employe recognition, he might at least be thankful.

It is meaningful that the questions in this letter show concern for the district's machinery of administration. This love of administrative organization for its own sake must have an affinity for or perhaps be derived from fondness for actual machines. It may be well and good for mining copper, manufacturing automobiles or motion pictures, distributing milk or gasoline, or building a skyscraper or bridge. But what about the ends sought in schools, in particular the school district in which this clumsy letter was used to bludgeon a master teacher? Learning is a personal matter with each individual and it can take place satisfactorily without any intrusion whatever of administrative machinery.

In this connection consider this one of the twelve self-righteous questions: 'Are children required to participate in all subjects regardless of their personal mood at the time it (sic) is scheduled?' This administrative dictum that all pupils must uniformly and simultaneously switch their attention in a lockstep from one subject to another throughout each day on a fixed schedule is the prevailing fashion in schools I have observed during the past 15 years. Here is administrative intrusion with a vengeance; each pupil must be stretched or suffer lopping off of one end or the other to fit the administrative Procrustean bed.

The public ought to be better informed of this lockstep procedure, for it is one of the worst possible situations for learning. When a youngster is interested in a particular subject, he should be encouraged and left free to ignore all else for the time being. Under this treatment he will learn better

111

at the time and will gain confidence and initiative and broaden and deepen his interests.

The point in one of the questions about having pupils 'perform operationally' in a way that adjusts them to their next year's teachers seems rather verging on a demand for miracles. Perhaps here again is the inevitable frustration of a cherished fantasy: even the master teacher is not an Angel; for this she must be spanked and sent on her Migrant way.

If this interprets the letter correctly--and I can make nothing else out of it--we are in pure fantasy land like W. S. Gilbert's Barataria, where the government is 'a despotism strict combined with absolute equality.' Except that this is real life and another teacher has joined the millions of past years who have suddenly found their employers uncomprehending of good work, incapable of appreciating the awakening of youngsters to the wonders of learning, and heedlessly demonstrating their incapacity to give and receive good faith in working relations. While Teacher Kelly's 'superiors' wallowed in all this innuendo and covert purpose, they still were in the act of giving her tenure, and at the same time complaining about the ethics of someone other than themselves. Yet this is not from one of Gilbert's librettos. Still, this is a fair sample of how thousands of teachers are treated every year except for the granting of tenure.

Chapter 15

ETHICS: THE LONG ARM

The fact that I engaged in picketing and other strike activity during a considerable part of 1959 has only accidental relation to my subject in this book. This period of crisis in my own economic survival happened at the same time Teacher Harry Elliott deliberately sacrificed his career and the slight modicum of economic security he enjoyed under the teacher tenure law. This coincidence gave me a vivid sense of the meaning of union brotherhood. He made this sacrifice by exercising his citizen's right to comment publicly on public matters. He impudently ignored the great democratic principle enunciated by Superintendent Downs that on becoming a teacher one must 'relinquish the role of a citizen-parent.' He was soon punished and put in his place for this arrogance.

Harry Elliott was a faculty member of a small junior college in a sparsely populated district. Being energetic and fearless, and having a lively interest in public affairs, he initiated a series of forum discussions of the local community's current public affairs. This was part of the adult education program of the college. He served as moderator of the discussions.

This was many miles from where I was on strike. I did not know of Teacher Elliott's existence until some months later. This was well, for after the strike I was more free and financially able to travel to meet this teacher and hear his story first hand. Also my own recent occupational jeopardy made me more sensitive to his. His conflict with the Educational Establishment began when he announced that the next topic of forum discussion would be the community's schools. Controversy arose at once and soon became of interest to the press. From that time my information accumulated rapidly, from newspaper stories and editorials, magazine articles, published statements by educational organizations and individuals, a 30-page mimeographed statement by Teacher Elliott, his letters published in the local newspaper of his community, and my lengthy conversations with him.

This is another instance, like that of Professor Darrell, of a teacher who emerged from the fray bloody of head but unbowed. There was some ultimate redress of immediate economic loss, but there was also a record barring him from advancement in a teaching career of service to the young and the civic life of his community.

Teacher Elliott planned these weekly forum meetings with care. He sought to involve as many citizens as possible in the discussions. His basic proposition was 'that truth can best be determined and basic decisions can best be made only after extensive and rigorous conflict of personal opinion.' In a statement Jan. 7, 1959 he stated the following conditions necessary to assure profitable results from such conflict of opinion; these conditions 'must have prevailed prior to and during the meeting.'

1. The problem or problems must be defined.

2. The persons involved must have courage to speak and act.

3. The persons concerned must be free and have a spirit of freedom, independence, and decency.

4. Persons entering the conflict must have facts pertaining to the problem and must have done considerable thinking, both of which are prerequisites to the formation of intelligent opinion.

These conditions laid down by Teacher Elliott suggest that he was well qualified to conduct a public forum; this is confirmed in my judgment by my subsequent close personal acquaintance with the man. He has proved his competence as a parliamentarian in the rough and tumble of political controversy.

Much more than that is implicit, however, in the above rules of discussion he promulgated and acted upon. These rules embody much of the essence of civil conduct and civic responsibility. Consider for a moment the last of his four conditions. A nation of free persons cannot exist unless, at an absolute minimum, this rule is practiced diligently by at least enough citizens to leaven the entire mass of the electorate.

114

A friend of mine wrote in a letter an account of his observing the British Parliament in action in June, 1967. The Prime Minister, himself a member of Parliament, appeared to answer questions, many of which were hostile. My friend wrote: 'Although the majority of the pointed questions thrust at him were by Tory (conservative) and Liberal (a small center party) M. P.'s, all the bombs were by no means from the loyal opposition. Sometimes the P. M.'s own Labour Party members asked Mr. Wilson some accusatory questions. He fended them without hostility, with dignity, and with respect. It is part of the Parliamentary game.'

This soft-spoken Teacher Elliott, of mien appropriate for presiding over an assemblage, holds a steady eye and calm manner in debate; and I have not seen any sign of fear in him under any circumstances. Several years after his collision with The Treatment he remarked casually, with his slight trace of southern dialect, 'I just do what I think is right and accept whatever the consequences are.'

With these ground rules laid down the forum sessions covered such topics of general public interest as fluoridation of water, a local city council election, and initiative propositions on the state election ballot. Through the local newspaper Teacher Elliott announced, on Dec. 24, 1958 and Jan. 7, 1959, plans for a forum series on public education. He listed specific suggestions for citizens to consider in seeking to become better informed. Among these were:

1. Institutions being used extensively for purposes other than those intended, i.e., overemphasis of recreation in schools.

2. Disrespect for and distrust of person or persons in authority.

3. A person or persons in authority under whom one could not work or learn without loss of personal dignity or integrity.

4. A system in which informing is encouraged (usually subtly), resulting in mutual distrust, apathy, and disgust on the part of many participants.

5. Absence of clearly defined and accepted standards or the

existence of 'facade' standards; that is, written or published standards and principles for show purposes, which nobody dares or cares to live by or follow.

6. Obviously unwise assignment of personnel.

7. No responsible delegation of authority so that members are uncertain of their relationship with other members of the organization.

8. Absence of a reasonable degree of pride in the organization.

9. A rapid turnover of personnel--the most easily perceived, surest indication of poor conditions.

(This 'surest indication of poor conditions' has always been widespread among school teaching staffs. An annual turnover of 25 per cent and more is common, as mentioned in Chapter 18 of this book.)

10. Absence of a clear and known personal philosophy or set of principles (about education) on the part of the staff.

11. Persons in authority very unwilling to make decisions and very willing to 'pass the buck.'

These topics, he carefully stated, were suggestive and not binding or limiting. The reader no doubt perceives that Teacher Elliott was proposing a very frank and forthright examination of the schools.

During January, February, and March his letters continued in the newspaper about the forum, mingling announcements about coming programs with interest-stirring accounts of the progress of the sessions; he also maintained that the forum was not a medium for reforming the schools but only a means of informing the citizenry; and that they should take action as they saw fit.

A basic assumption guiding plans for the program, he declared, was that the people 'either want or have a reasonable school situation over which they have adequate control.' He admonished the citizens, 'You are strongly urged either to support fully or reform that which the examination reveals.'

Readers will realize that local school administrators would be concerned about this project. These officials would feel that any such discussion as this should be from their initiative and that they should lay down the terms on which it should be conducted.

They did not sit on their hands. Even as the forum programs got under way in January, 1959 Teacher Elliott's superintendent, Administrator James Swan, appealed to the State Association for help. Teacher Elliott may have felt that he also had a right to expect some support from this organization. He had been active in it for nine years. He had organized or helped to organize two district teacher associations, had served as president of one of them, had been for five years a representative of the association's council in his 20-county section of the State, and three years a director in this section. He had organized a credit union for the 20-county section. However in 1957, more than a year prior to the forum project, he had needed help from the association and found it wanting.

On this earlier occasion, receiving a warning that his job was in jeopardy, he had appealed to this organization which he had served so actively and ably. He was told promptly that it could do nothing to help him save his job. Reemployment at that time would give him tenure. His employers had given him no warning or criticism. It is clear what the bar to association help was: the management prerogative to hire and fire at will. His local association and other friends helped him to save his job and secure tenure.

This is one of many incidents which have convinced me that in applying their code of professional ethics the schoolmen follow a strictly 'hands off' policy with respect to administrative prerogative of controlling jobs. Administrator Swan's cry of distress was another matter. This was not an administrator about to wreck a teacher's career; it was a teacher making an administrator uneasy. The association responded promptly. This gives weight to a complaint of some teachers that the association helps administrators but not teachers.

A few days after Teacher Elliott's first letter about his forum on Dec. 24, 1958, the association's Professional Ethics Commission asked him to tell about a difficult problem in his district which the local association had solved while he was its president. Administrator Lawrence Tracy, chairman of this commission, wrote Elliott that he wanted to use this case as an example of good operations. Elliott and a fellow

117

teacher spent a lengthy session with the commission early in January, 1959. The commission, Elliott said afterwards, paid high compliment for the manner in which Elliott's local handled the difficult case under his leadership.

On the day after this meeting the commission called Elliott again on another matter. They asked him if he knew he had violated the Code of Ethics in one of his published letters about the Forum. Elliott learned that Administrator Kurt Urquhart of his community had sent the commission a copy of this letter and had complained that it was 'unprofessional.'

The commission warned Elliott he might jeopardize his future by writing further letters for the public. He said they suggested he have somebody else in his community write the critical comments and draw the conclusions from the forum meetings. Teacher Elliott also learned of the commission's receiving the call for help from Administrator Swan.

Following are portions of Elliott's letter which disturbed the administrators and brought on his head the commission's condemnation. Referring to discontent in the schools, Elliott said, 'Many of us who teach have long been critical of the situation--but our voices have barriers.' He alluded to public apathy and to control of school boards by school administration, and he questioned whether the public 'would recognize a good school system if it saw one.'

'We might ask,' he wrote, 'why the individual classroom teacher hesitates to raise his voice. But you will remember, of course, that the teacher's job depends on his administrative head. And it is at this point that integrity and starvation collide.'

Teacher Elliott told the commissioners that his interpretation of ethics did not agree with theirs, that their organization 'used professional ethics to smooth things over,' and that it 'did not cure problems, it simply quieted them and left them to simmer.' Thus overnight Elliott's role had changed--yesterday a hero, today an outcast.

About two months later, on March 11, 1959, before I heard of this case and while I was on strike, Teacher Elliott declared in another letter in the newspaper that the educational association has a 'long arm' and that it can permanently affect the job opportunity of any teacher. This recalls Teacher Carmen Thomas' statement 'they all line up against you.'

The association conducted a hearing on Sept. 1-3, 1959 on

Teacher Elliott's alleged unprofessionalism. It recommended his dismissal, declaring there were unethical statements in his published letters. During the subsequent Superior Court hearing on Oct. 6-22, 1959, Teacher Elliott's attorney cited the following passage in the Code of Ethics handbook of the association, supporting Elliott's reference to the group's 'long arm':

'But there is another way in which a teacher's career could be ended by violation of ethical principles, even though no revocation was involved. This is by the investigative procedures of the (state association's) ethics commission, whose negative report can make re-employment almost impossible.'

Administrator Martin Vernon, an association official, said he was not familiar with this passage. His counsel, the district attorney, said the passage was not in his copy of the handbook. Court recessed to allow parties to the case to determine which edition of the handbook was in force when Teacher Elliott wrote the letters.

There was no explanation of how the two copies of the same edition (copyright 1955) differed in their contents.

This incident and this whole case as well, raise serious questions of enforcement of such so-called ethical rules; even a high official of the organization was not fully informed of them. For more than 30 years I have been close to the schools of the State in which these incidents occurred, and I do not remember ever seeing a copy of the handbook on ethics, or observing any teacher display familiarity with it. Seldom have I known of a teacher's showing awareness of its existence.

It is curious that thousands of teachers, through the years, have been subject to loss of livelihood through violation of rules of so-called ethics of which they are not informed. I am prompted to say 'so-called' partly because this neglect to inform members of the rules the association presumes to require them to obey is a poor example of ethics. One may find an even greater ethical flaw in this private organization's assumption of such far-reaching power over public employes whose first responsibility is to the public.

A final judgment of this case requires consideration of the effect of those forum sessions on the community. This was an educational project of Teacher Elliott. I have not talked with the people of that community about what values the forum

119

gave them; but I venture some relevant inferences.

I spent a good many years in sparsely populated communities such as the one in which Teacher Elliott conducted the forum. I have seen the people in such communities respond to such meetings. Activities of this kind bring the people together in constructive action. They are events to which people look forward and which they talk about and think about afterwards, and remember a long time.

People in small isolated communities attend almost any kind of meeting as something unusual, a break from the usual daily routine. I have experienced this as a youngster and as an adult. I still remember many such meetings. In youth they leave a lasting impression. There was a series of meetings in a rural Kansas community of my boyhood for conducting a sort of informal cooperative buying project. Citizens unaccustomed to speaking in groups did speak there with unconscious assurance.

It is inevitable that a good many persons gained important educational values from Teacher Elliott's forum. They became better informed about their community and its problems. Of greater importance, they learned something about practical and effective ways of attacking such problems. They experienced the exhilarating release of inner tension that comes to one when he speaks to a group, hears his neighbors, and reflects on the various points of view that come forth. They gained respect for each other, building community pride and community ties.

Still more important, they observed and took part in discussion under the discipline and restraint of sticking to the subject and resisting prejudice and mere emotion. This is basic at all levels in civic affairs and civil behavior which too few persons learn well and many not at all. Many persons in the community, whether young or adult, gained important insights and understanding which they will always remember, to their benefit. This is education.

Teacher Elliott's reward was to be cashiered. Any teacher rising to community prominence as he did incurs grave danger of losing his job--and his career. The people in that junior college district lost the forum and not long afterward they lost Teacher Elliott. Some perhaps understand, and others may eventually understand, that theirs was a great loss which the community might have prevented if citizens had been sufficiently informed about their schools and more concerned about their own best interests. Perhaps some will grope for ways of avoiding such losses in the future.

Chapter 16

ETHICS, PROFESSIONAL OR PLAIN

Teacher Elliott's experience calls for consideration of the whole question of what is generally called professional ethics, especially in the schools. The obligation to oppose wrong and support right applies alike to all men, and equally in their relations with all other persons, regardless of occupation or any other consideration. This is the point that stirs in me a resistance to the adjective 'professional' or any other adjective for the word 'ethics.' The word is better, I think, standing without a modifier.

The Long Arm reached Teacher Elliott just as it reached Teacher Delbert Brown, who looked all the way across the Continent to find another job; just as it reached Teacher Joel Conway who quit teaching because he could not find another job in his State and to whom it was profitless to look further; and Teachers Susan Prescott and Wanda Vinton who went further away than Brown for teaching jobs; Teacher Clinton Yearington, who found another means of livelihood for the time being as a State Legislator; Teacher Donald Xerxes who crossed the Continent at least twice and who has been earning a living for himself and his family at one non-teaching job after another.

These are actual persons, all of them, and all devoted, able teachers; but the Long Arm reached them; and it is not every teacher who can carry on a battle for survival for a year or a decade while incurring the extra effort and expense of defense, especially with no income. The Long Arm can reach any teacher in this Nation.

The American Civil Liberties Union intervened in Teacher Elliott's struggle, and the American Federation of Teachers, an AFL-CIO affiliate, supported him. The Superior Court found him guilty of unprofessional conduct. His school board fired him on Feb. 3, 1960 by a 4-1 vote. This was almost a year after my strike began. This was the high point for the prosecution. The State Association sought revocation of his teaching credential. The State Department of Education refused to revoke it. The State Appeals Court reversed the Superior Court decision against Teacher Elliott and was upheld by the State Supreme Court.

Whereupon this teacher who had assumed that the right to disagree really belongs to teachers as well as to others returned peacefully in September, 1962 to his school. Local citizens there, many of whom had supported him, reached into their pockets for the tax money to pay salary arrears for the two and a half years he had not been teaching while his case was going through the courts. He had need of this money after supporting his family as best he could during those years.

So ended this case. There are further considerations of ethics--a person's proper relations with and conduct toward his fellow men. On the issue of management prerogative the lines have been drawn, in the economy of the Western World, since the dawn of the industrial revolution. This issue has been fought continuously and bitterly, to a great deal of bloodshed, for 200 years; but the prerogative has never been really challenged in the schools.

Problems of human rights are involved in all phases of this struggle. These are ethical problems. School men, then, should be acquainted with that branch of human inquiry which is called Ethics (without an adjective). Men have pondered on problems of man's conduct since antiquity; the basic principles were enunciated by men of antiquity. Awareness of the principles is not uncommon, but true understanding is not easy to find, and their right application to specific situations is rarer still; for this requires wisdom about human nature, wisdom born of thought, experience, and just purpose, and the courage and integrity to base one's conduct on one's best understanding of ethical principles.

Were the educators ethical in demanding that Teacher Elliott surrender freedom of speech and that he conform, on pain of dismissal and revocation (as they intended) of his teaching credential if he refused? This stricture against him is a stricture against all teachers. As the schoolmen's ethical canons are stated, almost any act of any teacher in the daily affairs of life and work can be construed, to suit a particular purpose, as ethical or unethical. The punishment should fit the crime, as the Emperor in THE MIKADO realized. How serious must an act condemned as unethical be to justify the ultimate penalty of banishment from one's source of a living--banishment either by revocation of credential or by blackball?

Consider the four tenets of the educational code of ethics which Teacher Elliott was accused of violating. They are too long to quote in full here, but the essence is as follows:

1. The teacher endorses the principle that the profession must accept responsibility for the conduct of its own members.

2. The teacher exercises his right to participate in the school democratic processes which determine policy.... Once policy is determined, he supports it.

3. The teacher conducts school affairs through the established channels of the school system.

4. The teacher criticizes with discretion, knowing that only that criticism is valid which stems from a desire to improve the educational process and which is directed at issues rather than personalities.

Teacher Elliott pointed out the obvious, that this code is stated in broad general terms, and that 'its contents could be as easily and justifiably used to defend as to condemn my letter writing and the contents of those letters.' This is essentially the same objection Teacher Darrell made to the accusations against him. When phrasing is so loose that it is possible to construe at will many acts as either good or bad, evil forces are let loose, especially when the accuser holds the power to reject any construing that displeases him. When someone is harmed wilfully or irresponsibly in the name of ethics the evil is compounded by hypocrisy.

A witness against Elliott was reported to have testified that the code of ethics was 'developed by the teachers' of the State. It would be helpful to know who they were, when they did this work, and by what democratic process they were assigned this job. Why are not the teachers throughout the State schooled in the requirements of this code? This neglect is an ethical lapse.

From the actions against Teacher Elliott and similar actions against other teachers which I have observed, there seem to me grave questions of ethical conduct on such additional points as the following:

1. The obligation to support accusations with evidence.

2. Distinguishing evidence from hearsay, gossip, report, and unverified and irresponsible statements of all kinds.

3. Discrimination in evaluation of items of information that qualify as evidence, giving them relative weight.

4. Provision that evidence be weighed and judgment determined by persons absolutely impartial to the dispute and not partisans of any of the parties or of either side in the specific issues.

5. In case of guilt, penalties appropriate to the seriousness of the offense.

There are serious ethical considerations in other aspects of this case against Teacher Elliot, both actions and omissions. Omissions are mentioned because ethical conduct requires initiating action to forestall wrong as well as to exact redress for wrongful acts. For example, the complaint that this teacher was 'doing right but in the wrong way'; wrong because he had taken matters to the public instead of keeping them in the professional family, or because he had acted in his own name instead of hiding behind the name of some person not in the schools. It is questionable ethics to keep the public's business away from the public.

After the board's decision to attempt Elliott's dismissal another teacher was hired to take his classes and busy work was improvised for him. This is typical. Teacher Brown was set to work in the school library when he fell into disfavor. One may distinguish two points of ethics here: waste of public money in unwise assignment of personnel, and summary removal of established teachers from serving the young. Teachers Kelly, Isaacs, and others were similarly punished. These two points are important and to dismiss them lightly is an ethical sin of omission.

The junior college director released for publication a transcript of a faculty discussion of the issues raised by Teacher Elliott. It would be enlightening to know whether the association punished him for this breach of channels. It evidently did not urge his dismissal and revocation of his credentials. One cannot help thinking that channels are for teachers, not for administrators. The association took no position on the ethics of administrative intentions to fire Teacher Elliott in 1957 without warning or conferring with him. Failure to enforce ethical requirements impartially is unethical.

Why did the 'experts' spend money and time for the three-day hearing on Teacher Elliott's letters when they already had copies of them in their possession? Further issues of ethics could be raised in this affair. The fact that the educational hierarchy expends considerable energy trying to establish and enforce standards and procedures for adjudicating grievances indicates it is troubled by the dilemma of trying to afford some protection for at least some of its members. It is an utter impossibility to give teachers substantial protection in the face of management's blanket control of jobs. The fact that ethically questionable acts of administrators were consistently passed over while Teacher Elliott's acts in the exercise of freedom of opinion and of dissent were construed as unethical lends compelling weight to his contention that the ethical code is an instrument for holding teachers under the administrative thumb.

Also one can hardly imagine the hierarchy, being essentially management, voluntarily surrendering any part of its prerogatives. There is no end of evidence in human experience to support this thought. Once a system becomes established it is a sacred institution in the eyes of its beneficiaries. They automatically see criticism of it as something akin to sacrilege, as a clear violation of ethics.

This is illustrated in political matters. In an established despotism everything belongs to the despot. Others receive only what he chooses to give them. Certainly the despot would regard any threat against his despotic power as unethical.

There is no limit, none whatever, to what a privileged person may consider rightfully his. The astute Machiavelli mentioned the theory that a despotism is a desirable form of rule because the despot, having wealth and power, will be satisfied and will therefore more readily turn his thoughts to doing good for his people and being generous. This is a fallacy because any man's selfish ambitions are easily capable of becoming unlimited--absolutely so. History affords countless examples of this. Give a man absolute power in a state and he can as easily want more power and possessions as he can be satisfied and generous. Verily, if a man had absolute control of the earth he could become morose because of not having control also of the sun, moon, and stars. Give him them and he is still capable of aspiring to possess Andromeda and all the other galaxies.

There is a story of years ago, perhaps my rural Kansas youth, of a farmer who deemed himself modest in his desires. All he wanted besides his own land was the land adjoining it.

Man's reaction to power can hardly differ substantially in the schools from what it is elsewhere. It must be allowed that the fact that positions of power exist is evidence that an order of affairs, some kind of order, has come to existence out of man's efforts. And rock bottom truth lies in the statement of Alexander Pope that 'order is heaven's first law.' Equally valid is that power has its inequities, through man's imperfections and through the inevitable corruption engendered by power.

It must be acknowledged, then, that the order we have now in our educational system is infinitely better than no order. But like any other, this order is imperfect and some of the flaws can be corrected.

All of the ethical considerations of the case discussed here and in all of the other cases mentioned in this book strongly suggest to me that the greatest of all the violations of ethical principles was to promulgate and implement the code of so-called professional ethics.

Chapter 17

THE ART OF DEFENSE

Most teachers are easily overcome and kept silent during and after the process of being separated from their jobs. Few are skilled in defense. Few resist dismissal. Their usual course of action is to depart quietly and seek another job, very often in some other occupation.

A typical defense effort, in the comparatively rare instances of teachers resisting dismissal, is to stand on the issue of justice, as though this will rouse forces that will insist upon redress and reinstatement. In their idealism these teachers fail to realize the appeal to justice will almost certainly avail them nothing. Sporadic support is rare and ineffective, skilled support is unusual, and sustained support, the only truly effective remedy, is the rarest of all.

Although laws are intended to secure justice, there are multitudes of evils, especially the more common ones, beyond the reach of the law's long arm; and law gives teachers 'no rights whatsoever,' to allude again to Teacher Quentin.

If the dismissed teacher appeals to management she is in an individual bargaining situation and management, like any power structure, will stand on legalism rather than ideal justice. So far this book has shown management breaking a teacher's tenure without difficulty, jettisoning teachers at all levels from elementary schools through higher education, and using 'professional ethics' as a weapon to keep teachers subservient.

Now we come to a case of a dismissed teacher who was not naive about automatic efficacy of abstract justice, who had the courage to stand her ground, and who employed with virtuosity every available technique and instrument of defense.

This case had a great deal to do with my deciding that a

book should be written on the working condition of teachers. I was a newspaper writer assigned to education and it became my responsibility to cover the dismissal of Teacher Alice Adams. The case became news only because of her determination to fight the dismissal with every possible resource she could command, as a rank injustice to teachers. Such an attitude was almost unprecedented, especially for teachers in elementary schools.

My interest was deepened by two other cases of rough treatment of teachers which came to my attention at about the same time. Although both ultimately became news, neither was my responsibility as a news writer. One of these was the long-drawn-out affair involving Professor Darrell, 3,000 miles away, and the other deeply involved my personal life.

Teacher Adams' struggle was unprecedented not only for her persistence and resourcefulness but also because only rarely indeed have any of the thousands of school workers wilfully dismissed every year made enough resistance to attract public attention. Almost always these unwanted ones go meekly and nurse their wounded pride and misery in solitude. The persons who wield the power find this convenient.

I had had God's plenty of experience with teachers' working conditions but like most teachers I had never thought deeply about how the injustices and resulting harm to schools and youngsters might be unnecessary. These three simultaneous cases opened my eyes and forced me to think. I had not questioned the carefully nursed tradition that all school workers have the same ideals and goals and unselfish devotion to the young; that all are just one happy family of teachers. I had seen some teachers and administrators who did not fit this pattern; but this did not disturb me, for always there are individual exceptions.

I was disturbed, however, fairly often, by observing that many administrators in groups not infrequently showed an entirely different face. Also I became aware of an insensitivity in some of them, to teachers and their problems and to the young. Once when I was on a university campus attending summer session, another graduate student, a middle-aged man, saw me walking along a road and stopped his car to give me a ride. I did not know him, I do not remember ever recognizing him before or after that one occasion, and I never knew his name.

This man had a grievance and apparently he wanted to talk to someone. The burden of his complaint was that he had been a teacher and didn't like teaching because he didn't like youngsters. Therefore, since he had taken the courses of study qualifying him for administration he deserved an administrative position and was having difficulty finding one. He was an exception, of course, either because of his attitude or his lack of restraint or discretion in displaying it openly to a stranger.

The struggle of Teacher Adams dispelled many of my illusions, to my profit. Part of this valuable deepening of my understanding came from my observing the unanimity with which school officials throughout the State condemned her action and supported her adversaries.

Central to the main point here, however, is my observing in detail, step by step, the tactics Teacher Adams employed, one after the other, with cool patience and determination-- and the steady, consistent, and resourceful support and cooperation of her husband. I saw them adroitly turn the offensive of opponents into a defense which eventually crumbled into a rout. Yet there was no redress, but only vindication.

That is how all three of these cases ended--vindication, and only partial redress for one of them, Teacher Darrell.

As this teacher related the early part of the story of her dismissal in a statement to an Ethics Panel of a state teacher association I find it unnecessary to construct this part in my own words, presenting it instead as she told it. This was a year after she had been fired during massive dosages of The Treatment. The panel was hearing another case from the same school district. Teacher Alice Adams' factual statement covers the whole foundation not only of her experience but The Treatment in general, with many illuminating examples of the tactics.

I have omitted only a few passages unimportant for the purpose here, and made changes only to avoid indentification. Brackets indicate my explanatory insertions.

'April 27, 1955

'Statement to the Ethics Commission of the (State) Teachers' Association concerning the situation in _____ Elementary School District.

'by Teacher Alice Adams

'I want to say that as far as I am concerned the Panel is free to hand copies of my remarks to all persons mentioned. Such persons have a right to know what I say about them. They have the obligation to respond and I have the responsibility to support my statements.

'I hope the Panel will not feel under any restriction in releasing what I say to the citizens of the community. I shall feel free to do so, since the right of parents and taxpayers to be accurately and fairly informed about their school affairs is one that cannot be questioned on any grounds.

'I would also like to make it clear that I do not consider my appearance before this Panel as a hearing, or study, or investigation of the issue raised between the administrators of _____ Elementary District and me as a result of my dismissal last year. At that time I tried to get a hearing on my side of the issue, and was promised one by the chairman of the Board of Trustees, _____ . My resignation was based on that hearing as a condition. The Board of Trustees, however, decided not to honor the chairman's promise.

'After that I appealed to every possible authority and was everywhere turned down. One of the results was my resignation from the Teachers' Association. The damage done to my record as a classroom teacher, to my reputation as a citizen and that of my husband by those who set out to punish me for raising the issue of my dismissal has been done. I shall have to look for redress of that damage through other channels.

'I understand that this Panel is principally charged with investigating certain complaints of the teachers of _____ District against Administrator Laura Jones [Curriculum Coordinator]. I do not know what those complaints are. I am not interested in placing all responsibility on a single scapegoat. Rather I am interested in the conditions that are basically wrong in the administration of the district, which have led to a faculty crisis each Spring for the last three years.

'My experience as a dismissed teacher, I believe, throws some light on these basic conditions. I propose to tell you, simply and directly, what that experience was.

'I was dismissed on April 21, 1955 by the Superintendent, Administrator Albert Harris, in a summary interview in his office. I had no forewarning of his intentions. I had had no conferences on my work with him or his assistants.

'In that interview my superintendent gave as his reasons for firing me that the Trustees thought I was too old to teach; that all my supervisors of the last six years had entered adverse criticism in my files; that I was undemocratic; that other teachers had complained that I did not get along with them; that my principal, Administrator Oliver Newton, didn't want me any longer; that I didn't know how to teach.

'The Principal called me to his office to assure me that he had not recommended my dismissal. The other reasons, given by the superintendent singly and taken together, were a damaging reflection on my professional record. I determined that these reasons should not stand in the record.

'My efforts to obtain a hearing, and to bring into the open what facts or reasoning really lay behind the superintendent's decision, led me, my family, and my friends into an investigation that has lasted a year. From that investigation, supported by documents and sworn statements, we have concluded that my experience with _____ School District administrators, leading up to and following my dismissal, included but was not limited to the following incidents:

'1. Before the close of the school term in June, 1954 I was handed a list of my seventh grade pupils for the fall term. ...The selection of this particular group of pupils and the compilation of the list was made by the Curriculum Coordinator....In that class I was assigned 15 pupils who were rated as '4's'--that is, children who were two or more grades below their normal accomplishment or achievement level. Due to transfers this number was decreased to 13. This implied behavior as well as academic problems. It was the rule of the school that no class was to have more than three '4's.' I had 33 children in the class.

'2. Late in the Fall of 1954 a pupil of mine, a girl, went to an administrator (the testimony shows that this was the Curriculum Coordinator) to ask that she be transferred from my class. The girl was told to get the signatures of other pupils on a petition asking for transfers out of my class. Fifteen children were induced to sign the petition. It was filed in my record for later use. No administrator discussed this incident with me. I was not informed of the children's complaints. I discovered all this months later when the Superintendent told the Board that there had been too many requests for transfers out of my class; no doubt he had as his proof this secret petition.

131

'3. The Superintendent stated to me that other teachers had given him adverse criticism of me. He accepted this criticism without telling me what it was or who gave it. He asked other teachers to criticize and comment on my activities, and then used these criticisms against me with other persons.

'4. It was entered in my record that Administrator Newton, my principal, had attended 'several' parent-teacher-administrator conferences; that he kept notes of these conferences; and that the notes showed clearly that I do not know how to work with parents. The Principal did not attend 'several' conferences of this nature. If he filed notes on them as authentic, first-hand observations, he has fabricated those notes. The principal has refused to discuss this serious matter with me.

'5. The Superintendent laid before the Board of Trustees, as one of the reasons for dismissing me, this one: that sixth grade parents did not want their children enrolled in my class the following year. Who these parents were; how they were able to judge me as a teacher when I did not have their children or ever meet them in conference--these and other questions the Superintendent has failed to answer.

'6. It was also officially entered into my record, for the approval of the Board, that a county supervisor had evaluated my work, stating that I had poor control of my class. Since the letter of evaluation written by the Supervisor is confidential, I do not know what that Supervisor wrote to the Superintendent. But I know, on reliable information, that such a statement was not made for the record outside the school. My conclusion is that either the Superintendent told the Board a falsehood, or that there are two letters from the Supervisor each intended for a different effect. The County Superintendent of Schools refused to cooperate with me in getting at the truth of this matter.

'7. It is alleged by the Superintendent that I ignored the Curriculum Coordinator's repeated suggestions to me concerning alleged shortcomings in my teaching. Such suggestions were never made to me by the Coordinator. In three years of teaching she entered in my file that I had 'sleepers' in my class. I have been unable to get the Superintendent to specify where and when such suggestions were made by the Coordinator, or what they are about.

'8. The Superintendent also prepared the ground for my

dismissal by reporting to the Board that my county supervisor had urged me, at his recommendation, to take a year's leave of absence from teaching. This is untrue. I approached the supervisor myself about grants and loans for further study, and received some helpful suggestions from her.

'9. The Superintendent admits that my work was satisfactory during the first two years of service at _____ School. He has stated that only during the last year did I show signs of professional backsliding. At no time throughout that year was there a continuous and sincere effort made to discuss any of the foregoing matters, or any others that had to do with my presumed faults and shortcomings. Obviously the aim was to pile up the difficulties, real or alleged. The Coordinator is perfectly familiar with the operation of this system of compounded troubles. She has recently stated that she had no inkling of criticisms of her until she was overcome with an avalanche of them. This is the system that prevails in _____ District.

'The punishment that was decided upon by the Superintendent and his administrative associates consisted of the following:

'1. After April 21 I was excluded from faculty meetings. I was denied the opportunity to prepare a self-rating evaluation, such as I had made the previous year.

'2. I asked the Coordinator by telephone for the opportunity to discuss with her the reason for my dismissal. She refused my request.

'3. The Superintendent instigated and circulated the signing of a statement in the _____ School intended to isolate me from the District staff. This statement was signed by teachers, custodians, clerks, and cafeteria employes.

'4. During the last week of school ten children were taken out of my class and transferred to another room. This action was based upon letters the Superintendent alleged he had received from parents protesting against the emotionally disturbed condition of their children. I was held responsible for such alleged disturbances. Ten families were persuaded that it was unsafe for their children to be my pupils. The resolution to arrange these transfers was presented to the Board by Trustee Julius Brownell. I was not permitted to see the parents' letters. The Superintendent considers that they are private and confidential. But they were not too private and confidential to be used as cruel, unusual, and unprecedented punishment in public, with the unanimous consent and approval of the Board of Trustees. The County Superintendent of Schools refused to help me in determining whether any of my children were suffering serious emotional disturbances.

'5. The administration, it now appears, also resorted to doctoring a mental health questionnaire which I had been given by the office to fill out. This was a questionnaire to determine whether teachers could use the services of a psychiatrist in helping their pupils. There was no discussion with me before or after the form was completed. The Superintendent showed my answers to other teachers and got from them more adverse criticisms. He used these criticisms to belittle my judgment and later to actually suggest that I had evaluated 23 of my pupils as being 'mentally disturbed.'

'6. To answer some of my pupils' questions on classroom management we discussed the term in reference to a specific incident of two days before. This was a class-teacher planning for a day I was to be absent and an evaluation of class behavior with the substitute, the Principal. A statement was written on the basis of the discussion. Copies of this were sent to the Principal for his approval before the children took them home to show their parents. The Principal made no comment. Instead, he advised the children to destroy the papers. I knew nothing of the Principal's action at that time. The Superintendent later justified it on the grounds that I had 'forced' the children to write them.

'7. The point was made to the Board by the Superintendent that parents had complained that my pupils had learned nothing during the year. To bear this out, the Superintendent assigned the Principal to make an analysis of my class on the basis of achievement and other tests. That analysis is now in the record. It shows that the Principal made comparisons that are not warranted by the data he used. But a verdict was wanted by the Superintendent and the Principal delivered it.

'8. Some time in May the Superintendent sent a letter of 'recommendation' to the   College placement office. I am reliably informed that in this letter he states that I may be a useful school employe only 'under surveillance.' I am therefore recommended to future employers who are warned they will have to keep me under constant guard.

'9. The Superintendent has also now made it a matter of record that I have no favorable letter of recommendation from my previous employment at _____ School. This is untrue. There is a letter on record. Either the Superintendent deliberately ignored it or he made the statement out of ignorance.

'10. The Superintendent has stated that he received confidential reports from _____ District on my record there, and that his report shows that my work was evaluated as a failure. This is false. My written request for reasons of my dismissal from _____ were ignored, and at no time did any of the _____ school officials discuss with me or advise me on the alleged failure that the Superintendent has now been made privy to.

'11. These punishments were extended to rumors and charges by parents, apparently instructed, that I had prohibited the saluting of the flag in my class. This type of approach reached its climax when the Superintendent told third persons that my husband is a Communist. Others were informed that my husband and I connived to introduce union propaganda in my classroom.

' Looking backward over these events, I think it is fair to say that they point to a condition of an unhealthy state of mind and a lack of right values in school administration and in human relations. The result in my case appears like a conspiracy led by the Superintendent and abetted by the Principal first to prepare and then justify my summary dismissal.

'Needless to say, I am ready to retract each and every one of these statements the moment the persons involved come forward, deny them on the basis of evidence, and prove I am wrong. But up to the present all three of them have opposed a thorough hearing and investigation of these charges. This leaves me no recourse but that which I may possibly have under the law.

'I have held, and I continue to hold, the Superintendent primarily responsible for these conditions. Actions which he took directly, or statements made by him, represent a violation of nine basic points of the code of Administrator Ethics in Personnel Matters of the State Teachers' Association. The most glaring of these is the violation of confidence in the use of statements he obtained from the Superintendent of _____ School. [This was where Teacher Adams had previously taught.]

'But I believe also the Board of Trustees carries a share of responsibility for this state of affairs in _____ District. The Trustees admitted to the record very serious charges and allegations and even on occasion allowed themselves to be used as the instrument of the Superintendent's policy of punishment. I again have asked, this time through my attorney, Mr. _____ that the Board reconsider its actions and correct the damage they have permitted to be done to my professional reputation in the manner described above. I am waiting for the answer of the Board.'

The exclusion of Teacher Adams from faculty meetings carries a reminder that Teacher Jasper's colleagues could not remain neutral. Teacher Adams told me that a year or two after she had been cashiered, in the school office while she was on a business call she came face to face with one of her former fellow workers. This former woman friend, with a look of glad recognition exclaimed 'Hello, Alice! It's so nice to see--' then she stopped short in confusion, her face flushed with embarrassment, her voice faded, and she shrank away.

She had momentarily forgotten that she could not even remain neutral. I do not know how far her professional ethics rating would fall for this ethical lapse of forgetfulness.

It may be surprising, and it is significant, that nothing came of this thorough report of Teacher Adams. Considering the long list of underhanded actions she attributed to various individuals, each specified without equivocation, and her adversaries named and identified in every single instance, one can only conclude that her statements are true; for if not any accused person of spirit would have responded instantly to make her eat her words. But no one challenged her statements or acknowledged wrong doing, either through error, or wilfully or deliberately, or through misjudgment or pressure or weakness or momentary lapse, or for any reason. And this despite the comparatively large number of school persons involved--administrators, the five school board members, the county school officials.

I do not know how to reconcile these actions with the Code of Professional Ethics. I can only interpret them in the light of my understanding of ethics. Teacher Adams' list of these actions is long. She regarded all of them as unethical. It would be difficult to separate and list all of them, but it might be profitable to see the more conspicious ones, each by itself:

1. The dismissal of Teacher Adams without warning or conference.
2. The reasons given, unsupported, as customary, by evidence.
3. The assignment of five times as many below-grade pupils as policy specified.
4. The pupils' petition instigated by the Curriculum Coordinator.
5. Alleged criticisms of unidentified fellow teachers.
6. Falsification of parent-teacher-administrator conferences.
7. Alleged but unspecified hostility of parents toward Teacher Adams.
8. Falsehoods about unfavorable reports and recommendations of supervisors and a former employer.
9. The Superintendent's 'surveillance' judgment of Teacher Adams.
10. The fictitious helpful suggestions of the Coordinator and a supervisor.
11. The mystery of the 'sleepers.'
12. The false report about the proposed leave of absence.
13. The isolation of Teacher Adams from fellow workers.
14. Summary transfer of ten pupils.
15. The fact of 'confidential' complaints of parents made known to the public.
16. Misinterpretation of the mental health questionnaire, and covert purpose of the questionnaire.
17. Refusal of the Coordinator and Principal to confer with the teacher.
18. The Principal's inciting pupils to throw away the papers they had written.
19. The Principal's false analysis of achievement test results.
20. The spreading of gossip and rumor.

This long list, together with Teacher Adams' entire statement, was received in silence and brought forth no response. If her words were false it was unethical to ignore them. This behavior of her antagonists and the Panel is interpreted fairly as confirming her truth. It also supports the view that the Code of Professional Ethics is an instrument of keeping teachers subservient, and that its promulgation and implementation were unethical acts.

I have read the Panel's report of that investigation. It contains no recognition of any relation to ethics in any part of Teacher Adams' statement. It does not mention her contribution to the investigation. The Panel found fault with all parties to the dispute over the Curriculum Coordinator--with her, the superintendent, the school board members, and the teachers. The only ones explicitly found in violation of professional ethics were the teachers who had rebelled against the Coordinator under the conditions described by Teacher Adams.

The others, and the Coordinator explicitly, were exonerated of unethical conduct. The Panel found that the Coordinator showed 'ineptness in the performance of duty'; the superintendent had withheld 'much significant information from the Board'; a board member 'violated recognized channels and methods for the conduct of school business.'

It would be interesting to know how serious these offenses were in the minds of the Panel, by comparison with the double dealings, falsehoods, misrepresentations, and slander alleged by Teacher Adams including those in the above list and not challenged. The Panel may have excused itself on this point because these offenses pertained to another incident, not the one under investigation. If so, one may think they were investigating the wrong incident.

Police do not loiter writing citations for parking violations while a burglary is taking place under their eyes. Or are ineptness and violations of channels worth a mention and a spank on the wrist while slander and unsupported accusations which undermine a fellow worker without his knowledge legitimate administrative activities?

Teacher Adams' challenge that persons she named were under obligation to respond went by default. No one responded. None ever required her to support her statements.

Certainly people do not like to be told about their errors and flaws and misdeeds. They try to bury these in forgetfulness but this does not do the job. The evils fester in their inner being and manifest themselves later in irrational actions bringing on further damage. This is infantilism and it throws an added burden on persons striving not to be so infantile so that some order and decency can be maintained in society.

Reminder of one's wrongful deeds is bad news; people have the infantile trait of holding the bringer of the bad news responsible for it, and punishing him. That is why at least some of them were angry with Teacher Adams, and why some may be angry with me for writing this book. The fact that the bringer is performing a beneficial service makes him an innocent victim. Ancient kings killed messengers bringing bad news such as defeat in battle, or insurrection in some distant province, instead of rewarding the messengers for their faithfulness.

Chapter 18

INSTRUMENTS OF DEFENSE

Teacher Adams' statement shows that she understood how
to defend herself. Of course there was no legal redress for
her. There was no means whatever of forcing her employers
to restore her job and professional character and loss of income. Indeed there was little likelihood of her finding a
place anywhere, with her integrity intact, in the public
schools. She has never taught in the public schools again.

What remained for her was to document and establish refutation of the accusations and statements against her professional and personal character. Her struggles to attain
these goals began with the loyal help of her husband, Mr.
Adams, immediately after her firing in the Spring of 1955 and
continued several years. One side issue which developed involved Mr. Adams in a successful slander suit against one of
the antagonists.

I regret the unavoidable brevity with which I must treat
this affair. The case is unique in my experience not for the
harassment of the teacher but for her matchless defense.
Few teachers indeed would make the loss of a job an occasion
for such a struggle. Few indeed would be resourceful and
courageous enough to ferret out and analyze and assemble a
mass of evidence such as Teacher Adams presented to the
Ethics Panel. Few would conduct a battle continuing several
years that could not save one's job and that would destroy
one's chance of continuing a teaching career.

Nobody concerned merely with his own selfish advantage
would embark on such a course. Teacher Adams believed
wrong had been done to the profession of teaching and the
young to whom teachers owe the most solemn obligation of
service. She sacrificed her career to oppose this wrong. The
action of such a person from such a motive arouses intense
hostility; for when selfish persons are unable to find an ul-

terior motive in an adversary they are suspicious and fearful of being over-matched either in subtlety or, worse, in integrity. It is acutely uncomfortable to have to acknowledge moral superiority in an adversary.

When Teacher Adams began her struggle to rehabilitate her good name, I was little more than a novice in the tactics of controversy. Hence I was a fascinated observer of her step-by-step combat against the destructive forces swirling around her. I learned much about resourcefulness, courage, and intelligence. It is my hope to record here as much as possible of what I learned. This is important for citizens in a democratic society; and our schools have a great obligation indeed to sustain and strengthen democratic principles and processes. I hope readers will bear this in mind as they observe Teacher Adams' actions.

Abraham Lincoln once in his early law practice gained a noteworthy victory in a criminal trial by a tactic which illustrates the skill and resourcefulness a determined person may use. A witness had testified that he had seen the crime by the light of the moon. Lincoln proved that the date and hour of the crime were during the dark of the moon. He avoided one of the most common and pernicious causes of failure: neglect to ascertain the facts.

Other teachers should gain useful insight by paying attention to the means the Adamses employed in their campaign. Instruments for such a struggle for rights are available in our political and social institutions. There is nothing mysterious about what they are. If a 'mystery' is involved it is the skill with which one uses them. Without presenting a catalog of these instruments, one may cite examples, such as careful attention to relevant facts; accumulation of documentary evidence; appeals to fairness and reasonableness of adversaries; bringing issues and grievances into the open; appeals to the bar of justice; appeals to the bar of public opinion.

This chapter is concerned with how Teacher and Mr. Adams used these instruments. We begin with the accusations against her and the problems she faced in coping with them. Her statement summarized the accusations:

1. She was too old to teach.
2. The Superintendent's secret file contained adverse reports on her by county school supervisors, which had ac-

cumulated for six years.
3. She was undemocratic.
4. Her fellow teachers complained that she did not know how to 'get along' with them.
5. Her principal did not want her.
6. She did not know how to teach and had poor discipline.

These accusations and others made in support of them when controversy developed presented Teacher and Mr. Adams certain problems requiring decisions:

1. Whether she should try to continue her teaching career.
2. Ferreting out evidence, if any, supporting the accusations.
3. Clearing conflicting statements.
4. Clearing the accusation that Mr. Adams was a Communist.
5. Clearing Teacher Adams' professional and personal good character.
6. Tracing the source of damaging statements made against both of them.
7. Securing retractions of unsupported damaging statements.
8. Informing the public.

This was a formidable program, basically, I believe, because the persistent practice of school officials in concealing evidence for the purpose or ostensible purpose of keeping the dirty linen within the official family gives free rein to irresponsibility and the loose tongues of gossip and rumor mongers. Since school management men have not been required to support with evidence the reasons they choose to give for firing a teacher, they can allege anything that comes to their minds. This situation not merely invites careless and irresponsible accusations; it makes them inevitable, for the practice is firmly established by custom and tradition and is therefore assumed to be right.

Teacher Adams quickly settled the first point, whether she should try to continue teaching. She would have liked to continue, but she resolutely thrust this preference aside, to fight against the injustice of the system, regardless of the consequences to her.

Another of the eight problems can be disposed of in short order. Mr. Adams filed a slander suit against the person who called him a Communist and in a short time, as lawsuits go,

142

the court awarded him a judgment completely clearing his name. This was necessary to him because he was a labor organizer and there were powerful forces that would have been delighted to disqualify him by perpetuating the slander.

As to the eighth problem listed above, publicity, Mr. and Mrs. Adams utterly rejected the efforts of school men to keep the conflict out of the public eye. They publicized the case by releasing information to citizens of the district and by cooperating fully with the press, holding back no relevant information from newspapers. Publicity was a continuing matter, as the progress of their battle from time to time brought concealed information to light and as the conflict occasionally reached a crucial point, making it of interest to the press.

The remaining five problems are interrelated. The first overriding need was to uncover concealed information. This concealment gave rise to gossip and rumors, causing additional damage to Mr. and Mrs. Adams. In such concealment each rumor became food for another, with tiny speculations blooming into mountains of fantasy to gratify malice and credulity. In this irresponsible state people are capable of perpetrating great damage on anyone, innocent or guilty.

All such fantastic shapes meet instant and ignominious death if the simple facts become known before emotions and violent impulse harden into attitudes.

The six damaging statements given for firing Teacher Adams were followed by others, some generated by gossip and rumor, others improvised to support the original six. We met some of these in Teacher Adams' statement. They will recur as we relate the events generated by the Adamses' struggle to bring light into dark places where facts might be hidden. As matters turned out the light sometimes revealed no facts where someone had said facts were hidden; and often this absence of facts was as significant as if some had been found.

Some relevant facts are available bearing on the validity of the six original accusations. It was alleged that Teacher Adams was too old to teach. This one ex-news writer confesses a certain diffidence about anything as highly personal to a woman as her age; yet I venture to testify that Teacher Adams was certainly more than a dozen years younger than the traditional retirement age of 65. Some teachers continue in the classroom until they are 70. Teacher Adams is a very active, energetic person. During her three years in that school district she had been absent for illness five and a half days. This 'too old' count dismissed for evidence to the contrary.

Perhaps it is not surprising the school management cashiered Teacher Adams with the customary insouciance regarding facts, considering that teacher resistance in such a circumstance was all but unheard of. Yet anyone acquainted with her might have stopped to ponder. This tall, straight-as-an-Indian blond woman, they might have known, could be formidable. Fear is foreign to her nature. Now, a dozen years later, her energy seems inexhaustible, and she is quick in her responsiveness. An adversary is well-advised to treat such a person, even though she is of warm-hearted temper, with respect.

As to Point 3, that she was undemocratic, no one came forth with supporting evidence. This count dismissed.

On Point 4, that other teachers complained of inharmonious relations with her, see her testimony to the Panel. Her colleagues had elected her chairman of the District Professional Relations Committee for two consecutive years. After she was fired, and especially after controversy arose, the other teachers did not dare to remain friendly with her for reasons the American Civil Liberties Union pointed out in the case of the cashiering of Teacher Virgil Jasper. The 'democratic' separation set up between her and the other district employes by administrative fiat had seen to that. Her colleagues with whom I talked then and later showed no hostility toward her, especially for anything that had happened before her dismissal; some are still friendly. Count dismissed: no supporting evidence.

Point 5: that her Principal did not want her another year. She told the Ethics Panel that the Principal at first told her he had not sought her dismissal. I have heard no mention of his denying this. Thus her testimony is set against that of the Superintendent, who did not sustain his other accusations. Count dismissed.

Point 6: she did not know how to teach. She challenged Superintendent Harris to support this accusation. He did well not to state how much and how often he had observed her teaching; he had hardly observed her at all. This count dismissed for lack of supporting evidence.

On the remaining accusation, Point 2, which I chose to

discuss last, that the county school supervisors had entered adverse reports on Teacher Adams for six years, there had to be evidence, since these reports would be filed somewhere. At least two supervisors were involved, one in each of the two school districts in which she had taught.

She asked the school district management to allow her to read the supervisors' reports. Refused; she was told they were confidential. She asked the county school superintendent for copies of them. Ignored. She suggested that the county school office might be suffering damage by misrepresentations of these reports. Ignored.

Teacher Adams discovered, however, what these reports said about her for the official record. There was nothing damaging to her in them, but the talk of damaging reports continued. Teacher Adams thereupon publicly raised the question: Could a supervisor have written two statements about her, one for the record and another for some other purpose? This question left her opponents the alternatives of admitting that there was a second, hitherto undisclosed, letter or of denying the existence of such a letter, thereby disclosing the falsity of the claim that the supervisors judged her adversely. They chose silence. This leaves the clear inference either that there was no second letter or if there was, its unethical surreptitiousness was too embarrassing to disclose.

This accusation, like the other five, simply falls for lack of evidence. Count dismissed.

Case dismissed.

Perhaps readers of these pages have observed in this brief account how Teacher Adams made adroit use of the instruments of defense and counter attack. There are certain basic principles in such an operation. The separation of facts from a mass of confusing statements and actions is one such principle; it is easy to understand, difficult but not impossible to perform, requiring skill, self-discipline, and courage, which one can acquire by determination. It is necessary always to exercise great care in distinguishing fact from rumor and supposition.

Teacher Adams demonstrated that the powerful impulse to allow emotion and a sense of outrage at injustice to becloud one's judgment can be controlled to the point that the injured person remains objective in facing his problems. With such control Teacher Adams refuted her opponents.

Our next concern is with the other damaging statements and actions that confronted her, which required the same objectivity. I have listed nine of these injurious statements and nine such actions which she had to challenge, refute and if possible trace to their source. There are others; it is hoped these will suffice. Readers may check these 18 points in Teacher Adams' statement.

The nine injurious statements are:

1. That with the connivance of her husband Teacher Adams introduced labor propaganda in her seventh grade class.
2. That she had no recommendation from her previous superintendent.
3. That she had stated that 23 of her 31 pupils were so emotionally disturbed that they needed psychiatric treatment.
4. A board member said in a public meeting that a mimeographed statement Teacher Adams had written to parents of her pupils regarding her dismissal was '21 pages of lies.'
5. That a supervisor attempted to persuade her to take a leave of absence, in the opinion that she needed further training to become an acceptable teacher.
6. That her principal had attended several conferences between her and parents of her pupils and found that she did not know how to 'get along' with the parents.
7. That a supervisor said she did not know how to control her class.
8. That she ignored suggestions of the Curriculum Coordinator for improving her teaching.
9. The Coordinator had reported that Teacher Adams had 'sleepers' in her class, but did not explain what she meant.

The nine injurious actions I have singled out were:

1. Her principal, without telling her, influenced her pupils to destroy papers they had written which she intended them to show to their parents.
2. The Curriculum Coordinator early in the school year had influenced 15 of her pupils to sign a petition asking for transfer from her class. It was months later that Teacher Adams learned of this, after she was fired.
3. She was assigned 15 pupils--almost half the class--who were two or more years below grade level in achievement, though school policy directed that no teacher should have more than three such pupils.

146

4. One year before the superintendent fired her his evaluation of her was higher than her own self-evaluation.

5. Ten of her pupils were summarily removed from her class a few days before the close of the school year without consultation with her.

6. Superintendent Harris pointedly ignored her in scheduling annual individual Spring conferences with teachers.

7. She was fired without warning, in violation of the Code of Ethics and school district policy.

8. After dismissal she was excluded from faculty meetings and other contact with her fellow teachers.

9. Superintendent Harris, no doubt giving way to vexation, referred to Mr. Adams as a Communist, a remark resulting in a court judgment against him for slander.

Whenever Mr. and Mrs. Adams learned of any of these actions one of their most effective counter actions, after verifying the facts, was to publicize them. They talked about them openly, informed the press, and discussed them with friends, individually and in groups, talked about them with their adversaries and other school persons, and prepared mimeographed statements about them for distribution to district citizens and other interested persons.

They wrote many letters to school persons, especially their adversaries, asking, and sometimes demanding information about or confirmation of actions or statements pertaining to the injuries done to them. Replies to these communications were sometimes helpful. Often the failure or refusal to answer was as revealing as a response, sometimes more so.

Teacher Adams' initiative thus forced her adversaries to take defensive actions, in which they sometimes revealed significant information. For instance it forced or helped to force revelation of the nine damaging statements in the above lists, and Numbers I and 2 of the actions. She was then able to refute the false and inaccurate statements and reveal the hostile actions to the public, such as the underhanded undermining of her relations with her pupils by the Principal and the Coordinator.

In the next chapter I shall give as much detail as I can on how she was able to break through the wall of concealment against which she was forced to battle. Just one more point here: Teacher Adams' struggle widened into an examination of general school practices relating to the status of teachers.

147

Her awareness of the extent of secrecy became more acute when district and other school officials refused her request for information of the salaries of all employes in the school district from which she had been dismissed. She carried her request to higher authorities, including the State Department of Education. Finally she appealed to the State Attorney General. After two years of effort she succeeded in forcing disclosure of this public information.

She began investigating the annual turnover of teaching staffs in the district and later in other school districts. She found that a turnover of 25 per cent, and more, of teachers each year was common. On various questions, as I have mentioned, she found channels that turned out to be cul de sacs: Teachers are told that professional ethics requires washing the professional family's dirty linen within the family circle; but Teacher Adams could find no washing machine in the family. She held fast to the view that teachers should have the same right other citizens enjoy to talk to the public about public affairs.

She would have none of Superintendent Downs' dictum that one should not try to be a 'parent-citizen' and a teacher at the same time.

I think it not digression here to suggest that Teacher Adams' long, drawn-out struggle for access to public information typifies the erosion of civic rights that has been a matter of lively concern especially since World War II. Of course. Public officials will eventually take away the rights of citizens if the citizens do not resist. It is a law of government, indeed of human nature, that men with power will arrogate more and more power to the extent people will allow.

When Teacher Adams was battling for several years to obtain information that any citizen has a legal right to know, why did not the word spread like fire that a citizen's rights were being flouted, first by school administrators and trustees and later by county and state school officialdom? If they did not know full well this citizen had the right to see their precious public records, then why did they not know it? They are supposed to represent the best cultural level of a community. What is one to say of a community if such confused leadership represents its best? These persons could have learned as elementary school pupils to have some responsibility for guarding the rights of free citizens. Few things are more important. This is a primary function of the schools.

This is at the crux of our culture, our way of life. It is

our tradition that basic individual freedom is the greatest glory of our Nation. Then this--suppression of public information. As a newsman I point out that for the press the issue is nothing less than life or death; for the press as we know it survives or perishes on the issue of access to public information.

There is every reason in all conscience and good horse sense to fight the suppression of public information before this suppression becomes entrenched and institutionalized. The greater success is to forestall a critical situation; it is far less destructive than to win plaudits by victory in dubious battle.

The adventures of the Ten Thousand, of Achilles and Agamemnon, of General George A. Custer, are immortalized in song, story, and legend, largely because of carnage in desperate situations. The exploits of these adventurers and thousands of others are bungling affairs by comparison with the near-absolute perfection of Lewis and Clark and their men. They forestalled desperate battle by intelligent planning and foresight and humane treatment of the people they met. Part of their reward for this perfection is that they came back alive after opening a new era; but they have been underrated ever since; there were no spectacular battles and the expedition did not cause the death of a single member of the party.

Citizens should cultivate a like intelligence and prudence to ward off dangers to their freedom.

Chapter 19

HIT AND RUN DEFAMERS

Teacher and Mr. Adams' success in forcing disclosure of the salaries of certain public employes was a public benefit which has gone unrecognized except among a few of their friends. Thoughtful citizens should be deeply concerned that such an occurrence could happen at all in this country; that public servants anywhere could have the arrogance to flout the rights of the people who hire and elect and pay them to perform public service.

The Adamses demonstrated that citizens can enjoy their rights if and only if they are ready to fight for them. They also demonstrated that persons who take the role of teachers are also citizens and may be parents even though Teacher Updyke suffered a setback on this score.

This chapter is concerned, out of all of Teacher and Mr. Adams' efforts and successes and setbacks, with her campaign for access to her secret personnel file and the outcome of what she and her attorney found there. Gaining access required breaking the wall of secrecy with which such dossiers on teachers have been surrounded--secrecy deemed a matter of administrative prerogative.

She soon found no hope of forcing her way into the precious secrets of this dossier by appealing to higher educational officials or the educational organizations. 'They all line up against you,' in the words of Teacher Carmen Thomas. Remaining was the appeal to basic human rights, guaranteed in the Bill of Rights of the Federal Constitution. Tnere is nothing in the Constitution excluding teachers from these rights.

Teacher Adams reserved court action as a final step if other efforts failed, Through the good offices of her State Senator a legal opinion was obtained from the State Legislative Counsel on the right of access to a school employe's file. This opinion, dated Oct. 20, 1955,* clearly stated the right of a teacher and her attorney to examine the material in her file. Following are the questions asked of the Legislative Counsel and the Counsel's opinion.

QUESTIONS:

1. Are the Personnel files which are maintained by school districts on administrators or other school employes matters of public record, and who is entitled to examine them? For instance, could a newspaper representative see them?
2. Are employes themselves allowed to examine their own records?
3. When school employes are rated by their superiors and those ratings are made a part of their personnel records, who has access to such records?
4. Does the law differ from one district to another on these matters? That is, would a unified school for instance have a different ruling than another type of school? Are the schools governed by local laws in this regard?
5. When there are filed accusations or complaints against any teacher and those accusations are made a part of the personnel file, who may obtain access to the files?

OPINION:

Personnel files of school district employes may contain various types of papers, each of which must be considered separately for purpose of answering the questions at hand.

Documents in which an employe is rated by a superior would appear to be open to inspection by members of the public at large and also by the employe, in the absence of contractual agreement to the contrary.

The same rule would appear to apply to a formal complaint against the employe by his superior officer.

It does not appear that a member of the public has status to compel disclosure to him of the contents of an accusation made against a school district employe by another member of the public. The employe himself may have such access.

So far as statutory law is concerned, the law does not differentiate between one type of school district and another.

*The author has a copy.

One might assume that school management would respond promptly to an opinion as unequivocal and authoritative as this. However, more than a year passed before Teacher Adams and her attorney were permitted to see the file. The School Board endeavored without success to secure from Teacher Adams a commitment that she would not bring suit against the Board for anything she might find in the file.

In June, 1956 the Board voted to open the file to Teacher Adams and her counsel, provided the Board's publicly supported counsel consented. Five months after this a local newspaper reported that the Board had finally decided to share the dread secrets of this file with her and her attorney. The newspaper said Teacher Adams' attorney 'had filed a letter with the board asking again that the file be opened for examination. An earlier request for such action was referred to the County Counsel's office (the school district's counsel) which had sent it back to the Board without comment.'

Thus left unsupported by its own counsel, the board finally gave way, and Teacher Adams and her attorney examined the file on Jan. 10, 1957.

They found nothing in it to sustain the accusations and subsequent damaging statements and actions against her. Teacher and Mr. Adams took steps at once to make this known to the public, in the effort to clear their names. They were never entirely cleared; almost seven years later, in October 1963, a Congressman maligned both of them on the privileged floor of the House of Representatives.

The negative disclosure of the file provided opportunity for persons who had been deceived into harming Mr. and Mrs. Adams to correct these injustices. They both wrote letters to their various adversaries inviting them to reconsider, in the light of the newly discovered facts which had changed the situation. I give here one example, a letter by Mr. Adams to a member of the Board of Trustees. It is a long letter, dated Jan. 11, 1957, the day after opening of the file. I quote the greater part of it but conceal identifying material such as names. Brackets indicate my explanatory insertions.

'Dear Trustee Cecil Brownell:

'In the minutes of the meeting of the _____ District Board of Trustees for July 11, 1955 there is the following entry: 'Trustee Brownell accused (Mr. Adams) of lying. Later Trustee Brownell referred to the letter (of Teacher Adams)

152

to Seventh Grade Parents as '21 pages of lies.' I was present at that meeting, as you may recall, and heard you make those remarks.

'At that time I elected to hold in abeyance the personal affront your remarks carried, particularly with respect to Teacher Adams. There were previous questions of fact that had to be settled. The members of the Board and the school administration were in complete control of the sources of information which allegedly supported the charges against Teacher Adams.

'Your publicly expressed charge that my wife is a liar has had to await proper consideration until such time as we might be able to break through the cloud of deception and deliberate misrepresentation that has covered the Superintendent Harris case.

'That time has now arrived. After nearly two years of considerable effort and expense, the record of the case is available to us as well as to the Trustees of _____ District. Practically all of it arises out of the efforts made by the district's administrators to justify Teacher Adams' summary dismissal, without appeal, in April, 1955. The charges thrown at her (and occasionally at me) could not be answered at the time because the Board refused to give her a fair hearing with proper procedures. They can be answered now.

'Following is the summary of the record which shows who was lying:

'1. Teacher Adams was accused of sending a vitriolic letter to the chairman of the Board, Trustee James Allen! This is a falsehood.
'2. Evaluations of Teacher Adams are supposed to show her serious shortcomings as a teacher during the three years at _____ ! The evaluation of the Curriculum Coordinator and Principal were obviously tailored to suit Superintendent Harris' plans. They permitted a deliberately false conclusion.
'3. Teacher Adams was charged with giving 'bad' grades to pupils who did not serve compulsory time at the public library on Saturdays. This is a falsehood.
'4. Teacher Adams was charged with failing to mention to _____ Administrators the reason for her transfer from _____ District. This is a falsehood.
'5. Teacher Adams was supposed to have left [the district

153

in which she had previously taught] with no written recommendation. Such a recommendation is a matter of record, and the charge is a falsehood.

'6. Teacher Adams' record at [the previous district] was asserted to have been one of continuous failure. This is a falsehood, as the record now shows.

'7. A county supervisor for [the previous district] was supposed to have filed an adverse report against Teacher Adams. This is a falsehood.

'8. It was alleged that parents of sixth grade pupils of _____ had requested that their children not be advanced to Teacher Adams' class on promotion. The record fails to support this charge, and it is false.

'9. Other teachers at _____ were supposed to have turned in critical reports against Teacher Adams purporting to prove that she could not get along with the rest of the faculty. This is a plain and unmitigated falsehood.

'10. The Curriculum Coordinator was supposed to have made recommendations to Teacher Adams for the improvement of her teaching. No such recommendations were made orally or in writing, and the assertion is a falsehood.

'11. A county supervisor was supposed to have made the suggestion to Teacher Adams that she take a leave of absence for advanced study as a way out of the serious difficulties at _____. This is false.

'12. Teacher Adams is supposed to have 'forced' her pupils to copy a letter criticizing an administrator. This is totally false.

'13. Teacher Adams was charged with using violence on her pupils on several occasions throughout the year, of many instances of slapping, of choking a pupil and of sending one home with marks on his arm. These are plain and unmitigated falsehoods.

'14. Teacher Adams' failure as a teacher was emphasized by the alleged fact that she was purposely given a class of 'well behaved children' during her last year at _____. The record shows that she was given a group of 33 children including 15 who were classified by the Administration as 'fours' or below-grade pupils with behavior and other problems. The fact that the school lost its own record of this transaction does not excuse the deliberate falsehood. I have a copy of that record.

'15. Teacher Adams was charged with having classified 25 children in her class as mentally disturbed and in urgent need of psychiatric attention. There is nothing in the record to support this, and it turns out to be a falsehood.

'16. It was suggested that Teacher Adams' problems arose out of her poor health. Teacher Adams' attendance record at ＿＿＿＿ shows absences of five and one-half days on account of illness in three years of service. The insinuation is a falsehood.

'17. The county counsel of ＿＿＿＿ County was induced to threaten Teacher Adams with legal action after she allegedly made off with school property and refused to return it after being requested to do so by the Superintendent. This is a plain falsehood.

'18. It was stated that Teacher Adams' file contained an adverse criticism and evaluation by her county supervisor. This is a falsehood.

'19. Adminstrator Newton, then principal of ＿＿＿＿, was alleged to have kept detailed notes of 'several parent-teacher-administrator' conferences which purported to show that Teacher Adams mistreated parents, used violence on children regularly and otherwise proved her incompetence in dealing with other persons. Administrator Newton never attended more than one such conference. The 'several conferences' never took place. The statement and correlative charge are false.

'20. A petition was supposed to have been received by the Board of Trustees signed by several parents requesting that their children be transferred out of Teacher Adams' class because of the emotional disturbance caused in them by the teacher. This petition was referred to by you in a meeting of the Board. There is not such a petition in the record and the statement is a falsehood.

'21. Letters purporting to show that Teacher Adams was guilty of surreptitiously using pro-labor propaganda in the classroom were allegedly shown to members of the Board of Trustees. Such propaganda did not exist and the statement is a falsehood.

'In a statement made by the Board of Trustees of ＿＿＿＿ District, of which you were a member at the time, this observation occurs: '. . . Intelligent debate is predicated upon firm understanding of both sides of any question.'

'Because of the handicaps imposed on us by the administrators of ＿＿＿＿ District, and supported by the Trustees, the statement of our side of the question has been delayed many months.

'In view of what the record now shows, I request that you reconsider your public remarks concerning Teacher Adams, and that you make a suitable retraction of them. I am also interested to know whether as a member of the Board of Trustees you intend to make a correction of record of the false and unfounded charges summarized above in order to provide Teacher Adams with the recognition of her services at _____ as a competent teacher.

'If after a reasonable time I do not hear from you, I shall feel at liberty to try to remove the discredit that has been placed on Teacher Adams' good name as a teacher and as a citizen by means beyond the appeal for fairness.

'Very truly yours,

'Mr. Adams'

Just as the school management appears to have underrated Teacher Adams as an adversary, it appears certain they also failed to perceive how formidable her husband, the author of this letter, could be. They may not know to this day of the many bitter controversies in which he has held his own in far more than mere local affairs. Perhaps the quiet, mild demeanor of this dark, slim man deceived them. This is not surprising, since men are indeed few whose background, like his, includes high competence in such widely separate fields as scholarship and public controversy.

Teacher Adams wrote letters to school trustees and other officials involved, whose actions, which could have been induced by the unfounded accusations, compounded the damage to her and her husband, and reflected discredit on themselves. She offered cooperation to correct the record and counteract the damage. Neither she nor her husband received any response, nor apology, nor even acknowledgement. After the letters came only silence.

This failure of response signifies a shocking deficiency of fairness and moral responsibility, a lack that is widespread among us in this age. The late U.S. Senator Joseph McCarthy is recognized as having set the pattern of irresponsible defamation which has been a curse on our country for a decade and more during and after his national prominence. While no person in decency begrudges him this distinction, it may be recalled that some of his predecessors and distinguished contemporaries followed a similar pattern.

The evil that men do lives after them, as Mark Antony

said at Caesar's funeral. One of the evils of our time is the example Senator McCarthy and some of his imitators, the little mccarthys, set for their fellow citizens, of irresponsible defamation in high places. Actions of this character encourage release of the base impluse, latent in all of us, to strike out irresponsibly against our fellow men and make them suffer for our injuries, real or imagined, of which they are not the cause.

Sometimes someone innocently injures another through being uninformed or misinformed. It appears that this could have been the case with the board members who had employed Teacher Adams and with some other school persons who became involved. Or possibly this could have been an instance of someone's being misinformed at the outset and then persisting in the wrongdoing through sheer stubbornness or because passions and hostilities are aroused.

A person's civilized course of action after he discovers his mistake in such a case is well known. He goes to the injured person, acknowledges his error, and does his utmost to redress the wrong.

Teacher Adams and her husband resorted to enormous labor and heavy expense over a period of years in a systematic and superbly skilled endeavor to ascertain the truth regarding the accusations against her and the evidence on which they were based. They were forced to do this because in the administration of The Treatment the standard practice is to conceal such information.

When they exposed the falsehoods they hoped for some efforts of redress by some of the parties to their wrongs. None was forthcoming. Nobody ever even acknowledged the wrongs.

For a comparison of this conduct I draw on Bernard DeVoto's account of a dispute he had in 1953 with Congressman Carrol D. Kearns of Pennsylvania. In 'The Easy Chair,' HARPER'S MAGAZINE, August, 1955, DeVoto said Kearns defamed him by entering in the CONGRESSIONAL RECORD statements implying that DeVoto was a Communist sympathizer. DeVoto sent a letter to Kearns showing that Kearns' insinuation could not possibly be true. He asked Kearns to enter this refutation in the CONGRESSIONAL RECORD. He waited for an acknowledgment of the letter.

Two years later DeVoto commented: 'He has never acknowledged it. In this instance at least he was a hit and run defamer.'* DeVoto was generously gifted with original con-

*THE EASY CHAIR. Boston: Houghton Mifflin. 1955. p. 209fn.

crete apt phrases. I acknowledge here my indebtedness to him for a chapter title.

Teacher Adams' masterly defense, as matchless as and perhaps more wide ranging than that of Teacher Darrell, could not salvage her job or career. The fact that as a teacher one has 'no rights whatsoever,' to cite Teacher Quentin's judge once more, is too great a handicap even for the most skillful and bravest campaigner.

Chapter 20

SOUTH PASS

I know of no way to determine how many or what percentage of school administrators deliberately practice The Treatment, how many reject it, how many abhor it; whether it is part of the content of the philosophy and theory of school administration studied by men preparing for school administrative careers. Most likely like Topsy it 'just growed.' School leaders have always been reticent with me on this subject. I have sometimes mentioned it to some of them but have never met with response that could go into a discussion.

An official of the association once remarked to me that not infrequently an administrator in the midst of a dismissal or preparation for one will 'panic.' I regret not having shown initiative in opening the subject to discussion. No administrator has ever denied to me the fact of The Treatment. Some have deprecated it by a brief word or gesture. There must be many who deplore it. In this they assuredly have my respect. What I have said in exposure and criticism of it is not for them but for whom the shoe fits.

The school organizations propose under their professional ethics code to discipline and regulate their members. It is well to wish them success. I shall await evidence of beneficial results in this endeavor. Since I cannot account, however, for their ignoring flagrant violations of ordinary civil conduct such as are cited in the case studies I have presented, I am waiting without optimism.

Perhaps this is enough on ethics, though there is nothing more basic, and on The Treatment. There will be no true relief from the deplorable situation of teachers until basic rights are established for them and these rights recognized and accepted by school management and the public, and enforceable in the courts if necessary. What are these rights?

The same other citizens enjoy as a matter of course, such as those the Bill of Rights guarantees; also the right to assume responsibilities and to work creatively and to earn a living in peace and reasonable security, to exercise initiative and leadership in improving the conditions under which learning and the growth of the young mind and spirit can flourish.

Present conditions discourage teachers from effective work in this fashion. The domination of school management over their every act and their means of earning a living forces teachers to the extremes of caution and fear. Creative work is next to impossible under these conditions; entirely impossible whenever management chooses to make it so, as for instance when the new administrative broom is sweeping clean. One of the surest signs of ineffective operation is rapid turnover of personnel. This has been a blight on the public schools from the beginning.

Thirty years ago one of the most prominent leaders in educational thought, Dr. William Heard Kilpatrick of Teachers College, Columbia University, enunciated a principle attributed to Plato which applies exactly to the working conditions of teachers.

'For Plato,' he said, 'the essence of slavery lay in separating the forming of purposes from the execution of purposes and lodging them in separate persons.'* In schools the purposing of what teachers shall do and how they shall do it is the exclusive prerogative of school management. The execution of these purposes is the duty of the teacher. If a teacher carries out any of his own purposes it is by permission, not by right. Management may interfere and stop the teacher at any moment.

Some persons have asked me to state a remedy for the flaws with which this writing is concerned. I shall offer some thought on this but it would be absurd to give a neat prescription as though one were omniscient. The necessary first step is to inform the public. That is the prime purpose of this writing. People should have the kind of schools they want and are willing to pay for. They should strive to be enlightened in determining their wants. They should have more sound advice from persons informed about learning. I doubt the value of advice from school specialists who speak democracy and practice authoritarianism.

*PROGRESSIVE EDUCATION. New York: Progressive Education Association. XVI, No. 2, Feb., 1939, p. 35.

The people should be aware on the one hand of existing flaws and on the other what improvements could reasonably be expected from correction of the flaws. Another step and I think a very promising one in seeking a remedy would be to observe how working conditions of employes in other occupations have been ameliorated. The usual methods of improving conditions have been the paternalism of civil service for public employes and the self-reliance of collective action for both private and public employes. I know of no reason why either or both of these would be objectionable for the schools. I have not heard civil service discussed as a remedy. School management has always proclaimed its abhorrence of unionism on the ground of some distinction between labor and professionalism. The essence of unionism is simply the organization of employes for collective protection of their means of supporting themselves and their families. I do not understand how this can be acceptable in some occupations but evil in others. People have a right to support each other in protecting their common interests.

There are of course many groups besides unions that use collective action to protect their interests and further their goals, especially economic goals, which are the rock-bottom concern of unions. There is no end of such groups: associations of doctors, lawyers, school administrators; Chambers of Commerce; the National Association of Manufacturers.

If such an organization were established to protect teachers' jobs it would have to exclude top administrators, for they naturally protect their power to control teachers' jobs and this puts them in opposition to the teachers' interests. This is the labor-management situation.

My suggestion of comparing teaching with other occupations with regard to stability and security is indeed brief and simple, but it is fraught with very far-reaching and fundamental possibilities. The comparison should be not with just one or two equally unstable occupations such as nursing or farm labor, but with the whole gamut of thousands of occupations of the Nation's 60 million or 70 million employes, including the millions in hundreds of occupations under federal, state, municipal, county, etc. civil service, and the 15 million labor union members in hundreds of fields of work. Such a comparison would not be a monumental task.

With this I think I have suggested God's plenty toward seeking a solution of the problem. Now for a few words on the necessity of reasonable economic security and freedom to teach. The 1961 law which gave Teacher Quentin the right to

a futile hearing whereas he had previously had no right whatsoever suggests that stronger laws might be enacted to make
teaching a more stable job.

If there is to be legislation citizens must want it. They
would surely want it or some other relief for teachers if they
perceived the prodigal waste and inefficiency which the existing conditions make inevitable. The most conspicuous evidence of this waste is the perpetual annual rapid turnover of
teaching staffs. The waste of money in training many persons
who never use the training or use it only briefly is serious,
but nothing to the waste of human resources by inferior education.

If a reform of the instability should be effected, it will follow growing public awareness and widespread discussion of
ideas by many persons. It is my aim to provide the public
some information helpful in creating awareness of the problem.

It was my thought in first planning this book to relate many
more cases of The Treatment than I have done, perhaps 50
cases, or more. It soon became apparent, however, that in
no event could I cite enough examples to prove any point
statistically. Therefore the number of cases is unimportant.
What is crucial is how the cases I have given relate to the
conditions which make abuse of teachers easy and desirable
to one grasping for his own advantage. The cases are not
isolated oddities and aberrations. They arise out of the
working conditions of all teachers and they show conditions
intolerable to most persons but the meek, and corrosive to
all who endure this lot.

The fact of the instability needs no proof. Everybody knows
it. From as early as I can remember, school people con-
tinually, and other citizens when occasion reminds them of
it, have cried out, 'How can we keep enough good teachers?'
I have sought to specify the conditions that drive teachers
out. It would only be cumulative to pile up more cases. There
are innumerable such cases and each is the same story with
minor variations. I believe millions of citizens are aware of
instances of school workers being done out of their jobs for
no substantial reasons. The very commonplaceness of such
incidents obscures their significance.

The tactics are perhaps not so well known but there is
widespread evidence of their practice. I believe many readers
can verify this by checking in their own areas the techniques

I have cited; but they will have to prove to teachers that they can keep a confidence.

Uncertainty of continuance on the job and absence of freedom from administrative and supervisorial meddling saps the teachers' energies and vitiates their initiative. The lack of continuity by rapid turnover makes development of a strong learning program impossible. The uncertainty discourages and turns away persons with initiative and individuality and with the desire to achieve for themselves a stable socioeconomic status, without which a genuine professional career is impossible.

My effort to show that this is a matter of major importance in education and to arouse interest in correction seems to parallel in miniature the efforts of Europeans, beginning 500 years ago, to find the most feasible water route to the rich markets of the Orient.

Columbus started the search for a westward water route that would be better than the perilous interminable one around Africa and through the Indian Ocean. His discovery of an enormous land mass barring the way to China and India was followed by some 300 years of searching for a way through or around the Americas. Explorers investigated every river emptying into the Atlantic, every inlet, every bay. Dreamers and geographers imagined deep bays on the Pacific side reaching almost all the way to the Atlantic or waters connected with the Atlantic, such as the mythical Strait of Anian.

The water route Columbus and numberless subsequent explorers sought was the Route to Cathay, Route to China, Passage to India, and finally the Northwest Passage. This was what Lewis and Clark set out to find when they started their famous exploration in 1804, paddling up the Missouri River 312 years after Columbus' first voyage. That was the end of the search. It removed the last hope that there was a natural water route across America.

Almost a generation later men found the only route across the Continental Divide which could be traversed by schooners, but these were only prairie schooners traveling not on water, with sails, but wagons, with squeaking wheels drawn by oxen or mules. The pass is a wide, rolling stretch of alkali and sagebrush desert in Wyoming. It came to be called South Pass. It was the nearest of anything there was to a Northwest Passage.

I offer my thoughts to the search for a South Pass to a most urgent need of the schools, namely stabilization of school work as an occupation. I think this Pass must be found before this Nation can secure and prosper from the riches of truly professional work in the classroom. Discovery of this Passage will require realistic, hard examination of the problem, open and free clash of ideas and opinions, analysis by many sincere and earnest persons, and acceptance of the facts discovered, and their implications. People must first want a solution. The problem, it must be assumed, is certainly possible of solution; but no solution can be handed out forthwith, like instant coffee.

It has been my endeavor to show that the basing of job tenure in schools on the unchallengeable right of management to hire and fire at will has made school work inacceptably unstable and therefore woefully inefficient and prodigally wasteful, especially of the better personnel. Teachers who insist on preserving their pride and independence of spirit depart from classrooms for other work, leaving the schools to the timorous and the ambitious. This goes far to explain the continuing chaos and havoc in the progress of learning.

I have shown how school management often resorts to trivial, spurious, and trumped up accusations in discharging teachers. This practice seems to stem partly from administrative insecurity. Teachers must love their work, else they would not tolerate the conditions. One wonders, then, why some of them give it up for the equally insecure administration. Perhaps those who do transfer to administration love learning and teaching less than the other teachers love them.

One of the attractions of administration is the power it gives over teachers, and the greater power over the young. This is a dangerous attraction, as are all positions of power. The fondly cherished tradition that all persons in education are firmly united in a great cause--a tradition often stated in such words as 'after all, we are all just teachers'--is a strong buttress to one's choice of school administration as a career.

I believe this tradition rests more on convenient policy than on truth. There is casuistry in the proposition that 'we are one big happy family of teachers' and that ergo our interests are all held in common. This doesn't hold as regards power, prestige, duties, goals, economic and other interests, and outlook on life. But the educational powers do not like this thought, and endeavor to lead the attention of teachers away from it.

The issue of an employe's right to a job lies squarely in the way of this tradition. This one-happy-family fiction helps to explain that school personnel institution I have called The Treatment. The right to control jobs, unchallenged from the beginning until the present--or at least until the New York teachers' strike in April, 1962--squares less awkwardly with the one-happy-family tradition when antagonisms are contrived between an all-powerful administration and a helpless teacher.

Administrative insecurity further explains The Treatment. The administrator's precarious situation sailing in a frail craft sometimes impels him to look to his own safety by lightening cargo lest he too go overboard. Here we arrive at the cases of Teachers A to Z whose misadventures are the main substance of this writing. Readers may be able to identify some of these studies. I see no reason they should not do so if they wish, nor why I should. I long ago pledged anonymity to the others.

The actions of some management men I have related call up scorn and contempt, along with chagrin for the conduct of men elected or employed and paid to be in the fore of cultural leadership. But culture is a word of notably loose meaning; after all, 25 per cent of the men in Adolph Hitler's Elite Guard held doctoral degrees. Men of high cultural achievement in any given field are not for that better than barbarians. This nation needs to decide what it wants its schools to produce, whether highly trained barbarians or civil human beings.

It is a truism that order is heaven's first law. Any kind of order, unless it is utterly destructive and so creates a void, is better than no order. Humanity has never devised a flawless order; and the flaws result in tragic loss. There may be many reasons why the schools have not corrected their flaw of faulty employment and personnel practices but I am convinced that an insuperable bar has been failure to take stock of the employer-employe relationship in all of its aspects. This is the stone in their garden of which they seem unaware as they walk the well-beaten path around it. Removal of this stone will require a determined effort.

I conclude with some comments on the difficult subject of improvement that might result from removal of the stone.

One cannot forecast precisely in this contingency of such wide possibilities. Removal of the insecurity and fear from sincerely devoted teachers would result in incalculable improvement in just about every conceivable aspect of public education. Inevitably, the prevailing fear and uncertainty affect all learners; for the young infallibly respond to the state of mind of adults with whom they are associated. Adults respond to each other in much the same way but not with such certainty and such far-reaching results.

It is safe to say that all youngsters in school are harmed by the deep fears that haunt the adults who guide their learning efforts. I believe that freeing school persons, and teachers specifically, of the fears that make them cautious and timid would release boundless energies for constructive, creative management of the learning programs for the young.

If fear were replaced with confidence conditions would be established for releasing a flow of ideas and enthusiasm, for wide development of diversity and individuality out of which would come limitless means of stimulating enthusiasm for learning, and unimagined acceleration of learning.

Such freedom would release among teachers a free, lively, and healthy clash and molding of ideas about teaching and learning, as teachers became accustomed to the stimulating experience of economic security and liberty to operate, each in his individual way, in his relations with students. Haply teachers and pupils alike would learn to be more objective and respectful in the face of intelligent dissent. This in itself would be a great educational forward step. Only when one has learned to welcome honest dissent and to respect the right of dissent, I think, can one know to the full the stimulus and exhilaration of the winds of freedom.

The existing atmosphere of the schools, stifling to the objective and eager clash of ideas in the search for truth, deprives the young of an essential element of true education. It leaves them unprepared to cope with conflicts of ideas and opinions when they meet them as adults, whether in the university or the hurly-burly of everyday life. If this is visionary, make what you will of it.

The American idea of public education, free and universal, is one of the most revolutionary enterprises in all man's history. If we cling to the basic concept of its purpose, to free the mind and spirit and develop knowledge, understanding, wisdom, and compassionate sensitivity to the facts of universal human dilemmas and brotherhood, we can release a force beneficial to humanity without parallel in human experience.

This good can be brought a long way toward realization if the persons devoted to learning and the attainment of wisdom, and to fostering this same spirit in the young, are released from the needless fears and restraints that shackle their spirits.

trial of, 119; dismissal of, 121-122; failure of effort to revoke his credential, 122; court reverses his dismissal, 122
Employer-employe relationship, 17-31
Engel, Senator Clair, Foreword
Engelhardt, J. L. and Fred, on school administration, 84-85
Engraving, copper and zinc, 22-24
Ethical problems, 122-126
Ethics, as a branch of human inquiry, 99; Educ. Ass'n's Code of Professional, 43, 51, 100-101, 118-119; questions of in letter to Teacher Kelly, 106-111
Ethics Commission, Panel of, 129-138, passim: report of, 137-138
Ethics Council of teachers, its advice to Teacher Kelly, 74-75
Everett, Administrator Hugh, 40, 77-84, passim; 87
Evidence, uses of, 11; in dismissals, 17, 36

Faceless accusers, 39-40
Falstaff, 38
Fictional names, 3
Fisher, Vardis, 83
Floyd, Teacher Wilma, 10
Frank, Teacher Edith, 45
Frederick, School Trustee Percy, 62
French Revolution, 9
Frost, Robert, 27

George, Teacher Freda, 8, 37, 45, 86
Gilbert, Teacher Ralph, 45
Gilbert, W. S., 80, 112
Ginsberg, Allen, 79
Goodwin, Teacher Orville, his chicken house 'office,' 101
GRAPES OF WRATH, 8, 33
Great Britain, on independence for India, 87

Hagman, Harlan L., on school administration, 85
Harassing, of employes, techniques of, 44

HARPER'S MAGAZINE, 157
Harris, Administrator Albert, 130-135, passim; 144, 147
Hearing, on dismissal, 10-17
Henry, Teacher Alden, 10, 101, 102
Hitler's, Adolph, Elite Guard, 165
Hostages and reprisals, as technique of The Treatment, 46, 56
HOWL (poem), 79, 80, 81
Hudson's Bay Co., 44

Idaho, State of, 44
Individual bargaining, 2
Industrial Revolution, 17-20
Informers, 39-40
Ingalls, Teacher Clara, 41
Instability of teachers' jobs, 3-4
Inverness, Administrator Loren, 40
Isaacs, Teacher Leon, 10-17; hearing on dismissal of, 10-16; accusations against, 11; simulitude of a trial, 11-13; 19, 28, 34, 36, 37, 41, 47, 61, 79, 84, 86, 124
Iverson, Administrator Grant, 37, 42, 43, 56, 58

Janitors, 45
Jasper, Teacher Vergil, 77-84; poetry reading group, 79-81; American Civil Liberties Union comments, 81-83; newspaper comment, 83-84; 86, 136,
Jim the Wanderer, 9
Job security of teachers, 17-31
Jones, Administrator Laura (Curriculum Coordinator), 130-154, passim
Journalism Division, expansion and collapse of, 94-95; abolition of, 98
Joyce, James, 83

Kearns, Congressman Carroll D., attack on Bernard DeVoto, 157
Kelly, Teacher Hazel, 10, 35, 45, 48-75 passim; punished by school board, 62; the lesson plan penalty and other penalties, 64-75; futility of petition in her behalf, 73; in star chamber session, 74; 79, 88, 102-112; letter from School Board, 104-112; 124

170

171

Typography

for this book

prepared by

Friden Justowriter